The Chronic Mental Patient in a Community Context

CLINICAL INSIGHTS

The Chronic Mental Patient in a Community Context

Edited by
RANJIT C. CHACKO, M.D.

Assistant Professor of Psychiatry,
and Associate Director, Community
and Social Psychiatry Programs,
Baylor College of Medicine

AMERICAN PSYCHIATRIC PRESS, INC.
Washington, D.C.

Note: The authors have worked to ensure that all information in this book concerning drug dosages, schedules, and routes of administration is accurate at the time of publication and consistent with standards set by the U.S. Food and Drug Administration and the general medical community. As medical research and practice advance, however, therapeutic standards may change. For this reason and because human and mechanical errors sometimes occur, we recommend that readers follow the advice of a physician directly involved in their care or the care of a member of their family.

Library of Congress Cataloging in Publication Data

Main entry under title:

The chronic mental patient in a community context.

(Clinical insights)
"This monograph has emerged from papers that were presented as a symposium at the 137th Annual Meeting of the American Psychiatric Association"—Introd
Meeting held 1984 in Los Angeles, Calif.
1. Mentally ill—Rehabilitation—Congresses.
2. Chronically ill—Rehabilitation—Congresses.
3. Community mental health services—Congresses.
I. Chacko, Ranjit C., 1948- II. American Psychiatric Association. Meeting (137th; 1984; Los Angeles, Calif.) III. Series. [DNLM: 1. Chronic Diseases—rehabilitation—congresses. 2. Community Mental Services—trends—congresses. 3. Mental Disorders—rehabilitation—congresses. WM 30 C5568 1984]
RC439.5.C49 1985 362.2'0422 84-24542
ISBN 0-88048-076-9 (pbk.)

Printed in the U.S.A.

Contents

Contributors

George L. Adams, M.D.
Professor of Psychiatry; and Director, Community and Social Psychiatry Programs, Baylor College of Medicine

Allan Beigel, M.D.
Professor of Psychiatry, University of Arizona College of Medicine; and Vice President for University Relations and Development, University of Arizona

Richard J. Carlson, M.D.
Assistant Professor of Psychiatry, Baylor College of Medicine

Ranjit C. Chacko, M.D.
Assistant Professor of Psychiatry; and Associate Director, Community and Social Psychiatry Programs, Baylor College of Medicine

Rosalind J. Dworkin, Ph.D.
Assistant Professor of Sociology, Baylor College of Medicine

Aaron H. Fink, M.D.
Resident Psychiatrist, Baylor College of Medicine

Efrain Gomez, M.D.
Associate Professor of Psychiatry, Baylor College of Medicine

Daryl K. Knox, M.D.
Assistant Professor of Psychiatry, Baylor College of Medicine

Pedro Ruiz, M.D.
Professor of Psychiatry, Baylor College of Medicine

Seth W. Silverman, M.D.
Assistant Professor of Psychiatry, Baylor College of Medicine

Introduction

During past three decades, professional and public opinion concerning the care of chronic mental patients has shifted radically. Community psychiatry, once heralded as the third psychiatric revolution, advocated deinstitutionalization and the development of comprehensive community based alternative systems of care.

Mental health programs have emphasized accessibility, appropriate services, a multidisciplinary team approach, continuity of care, aggressive case management, individualized program planning, and linkage to social support networks. More recently, the community support program (CSP) movement has focused its attention on psychosocial rehabilitation services, housing and group residential arrangements, supportive work environments, case management, and a greater and more sympathetic interaction with patient's families.

These changes appear to be highly desirable and attractive solutions to the complex myriad of problems that face the chronic mental patient in the community. However, despite the development of several successful small-scale models, community based care of chronic mental patients by large public mental health systems has been the subject of fierce criticism by mental health professionals, the press, and various lay groups across the country. Diminishing fiscal resources, interagency turf issues, polarization of treatment providers, inadequately trained staff, high rates of "staff burnout," and decreasing interest by psychiatrists to work in community centers have been cited as some of the reasons for the failure to accomplish earlier objectives.

This monograph has emerged from papers that were presented as a symposium at the 137th Annual Meeting of the American Psychiatric Association. The authors have carefully explored some of the major areas of concern pertaining to the care of the chronic patient in a community context in the six chapters that follow.

Chapter One provides a historical background to the issues that are discussed in later chapters. Drs. Ranjit Chacko, George Adams, and Efrain Gomez follow the major cycles of reform, and find that progressive periods have alternated throughout history with other periods in which the chronic mentally ill have tended to be neglected and confined. The authors explore the role of the patient, family, mental health professional, and society in determining chronicity and in influencing outcome.

In Chapter Two, Dr. Allan Beigel focuses attention on the most significant achievements that have been made in the care of the chronic mental patient during the past decade, achievements that have played a role in shaping public policy. Methods that will be used to finance the care provided, such as targeted funding approaches, prospective payment, and mechanisms for providing reimbursement to health and social service providers, are discussed.

Drs. Carlson and Ruiz note, in Chapter Three, the dramatic increase in young adult chronic patients, and discuss their impact on and demand for hospital services. The role of the public sector psychiatric hospital service is presented, with strategies for dealing with high readmission rates, recidivism, and linkage to community mental health centers and aftercare services.

In Chapter Four, Drs. Adams, Dworkin, and Knox report on a study of polypharmacy in five public sector clinics using chart data from 1,752 ambulatory chronic patients. They have found the rate of polypharmacy to be lower than that previously reported in the literature. The factor most highly related to polypharmacy is the diagnosis of the patient. A slight tendency for polypharmacy to increase over a one year period, especially in patients on long-acting neuroleptics and on lithium, is noted.

The importance of work experiences in the rehabilitation of chronic patients is discussed by Dr. Ranjit Chacko in Chapter Five. An innovative program model that provides opportunities for chronic patients to participate in work related activities as volunteers in a traditional clinical setting is presented. The program has had a significant, positive impact on patient outcome and on staff attitudes about the level of functioning that can be achieved with this group of patients.

In Chapter Six, Drs. Silverman and Fink provide a historical review of the increasingly complex and often ambiguous influence of the legal system on the care of the chronic mental patient. Civil commitment, the right to treatment, competency, confidentiality, and the right to refuse treatment are explored in detail. Landmark judicial decisions have a major impact on the delivery of services; but it is difficult to assess the overall effect of these varied and often contradictory decisions on the quality of care that is delivered to these patients.

This monograph highlights issues and problems pertaining to the care of the chronic patient in community settings, and suggests alternative legislative, fiscal, programmatic, and clinical solutions for overcoming barriers and providing comprehensive care to this group of patients. We hope that this monograph will increase the interest of psychiatrists and other mental health professionals in caring for the chronic mentally ill, stimulate research, and aid in the development of more innovative, alternative treatment programs and systems of care.

Ranjit C. Chacko, M.D.

1

The Care of the Chronic Mental Patient: A Historical Perspective

Ranjit C.Chacko, M.D.
George L. Adams, M.D.
Efrain Gomez, M.D.

1

The Care of the Chronic Mental Patient: A Historical Perspective

Despite nearly 200 years of experience and progress in the treatment of the chronic mental patient, the goal of providing humane mental health care to this population has not yet been realized.

Until the late 18th century, the mentally ill were confined with criminals, beggars, and paupers. The work of Pinel in France and Tuke in England led to the replacement of the prevailing concept of social deviance with a model of disease and illness. Pinel believed that the deteriorated behavior observed in these patients was not a result of their illness, but was due to the treatment they received. This led to his major accomplishment at the Hospital Bicetre, the freeing of the mentally ill from their shackles. Thus, a new form of "moral treatment" emerged that created small asylums, and stressed medical treatment in a warm, caring milieu. Under the influence of this humane treatment, the disabilities that had once characterized the chronic mental patient significantly diminished.

By the middle of the 19th century, as a result of pressure from Quaker groups in England, asylums became open and unlocked institutions. The treatment emphasized persuasion, rational discussion, and interpersonal interaction. Families were encouraged to visit relatives in hospitals, and reports of "cure rates" markedly increased in number. However, patients suffered frequent relapses and had to be rehospitalized. In the United States, Dorothea Dix focused public attention on the plight of the severely mentally ill and urged their transfer from jails and poor houses to state institutions.

Around the turn of the century, partly as a result of increased urbanization, immigration, and the industrial revolution, demands for institutional care rapidly increased, leading to the overcrowding and further expansion of state hospitals. Psychiatrists began to lose interest in and optimism about the moral treatment approach, and instead devoted their efforts to listing, describing, and classifying symptoms, and to searching for organic etiologies of various forms of mental illness. Optimism about this "new scientific approach" in psychiatry leading to the cure of at least certain forms of serious mental illness became a popular idea. The close relationship between patients and staff that was an essential part of moral treatment began to disappear again, giving way to a "dark age" (1890-1950) in the care of the chronic mentally ill.

A second era of reform began shortly before World War II, and was given tremendous impetus by the war itself. Public awareness of severe mental illness was heightened by the rejection of large numbers of young males because they were mentally unfit for military duty. The Marlborough Program, begun in 1938 under the direction of Joshua Bierer, was, to a large extent, developed during the war. The key points of the program were the therapeutic social clubs for patients, day and night care centers, after care, and rehabilitation programs.

After the war, English hospital superintendents led by Bell, Rees, and MacMillan, repeated Pinel's experiment by unlocking their doors. Simultaneously, under the influence of Maxwell Jones, Superintendent of Dingleton Hospital in Melrose, Scotland, the impenetrable social barriers between patients and hospital staff began to break down through the development of the "therapeutic community." Its main components were an open door policy, community meetings for discussion of daily living problems in the hospital (with the full participation of the staff), patient government or community councils, and planned occupational, recreational, and psychotherapeutic activities (Jones 1962).

At about this time, traditional patterns of care began to be disrupted by the introduction of chlorpromazine in 1954. The availability and widespread use of psychotropic drugs gave a powerful boost to the community mental health movement, and enabled large numbers of patients to be discharged from hospitals.

In 1955, Congress passed the Mental Health Study Act, which set up a Joint Commission for the study of mental health and mental illness. *Action for Mental Health,* the report of this Commission, was published in 1961 and advocated, among other things, that treatment of the severely mentally ill could be better accomplished in the community than in the state hospitals. This came to public attention in dramatic form through the 1963 Presidential address that proposed the establishment of federally funded comprehensive community mental health centers. In addition, short-term inpatient care and the establishment of psychiatric units in general hospitals were stimulated by the availability of federal funds through the Hill-Burton Act. Thus, the deinstitutionalization movement was the product of several factors that resulted in a major change in social policy (Pepper 1982): *1.* the discovery of effective pharmacologic agents that control the more florid symptoms of mental illness; *2.* the realization by mental health professionals that patients are able to achieve much higher levels of functioning when they are in normalizing roles in society; *3.* landmark judicial decisions and legal challenges to institutions that have made mental health professionals acutely aware of civil rights issues and the rights of patients; *4.* economic considerations prompted by the astronomical rise in the cost of inpatient care.

Ten years later, however, writing in the Editorial page of the American Journal of Psychiatry, Robert Reich called the care and treatment of the severely and chronically mentally ill a national disgrace (Reich 1973). He wrote, "Our present policy of discharging helpless human beings to a hostile community is immoral and inhumane" (p. 912). Yet Greenblatt (1973), in "Dynamics of Institutional Change," predicted that all state hospitals in California would be phased out by 1977. However, as we know today, the state hospitals continue to remain open and there have been dramatic increases in readmission rates, and problems with recidivism.

Six years after Reich's report, John Talbott (1979) wrote a similar editorial in the American Journal of Psychiatry entitled "Care of the Chronically Mentally Ill Still a National Disgrace." At the present time, the policy of deinstitutionalization is resulting in reinstitutionalization of patients in supervised residential care facilities, correctional institutions, and in the streets of our communities. Gralnick (1983), in "Deinstitutionalization: Origins and Signs of Failure," notes that patients in the community are not as well off as they were in the hospital. In addition, the mental status and emotional well-being of these patients are no better than those of patients confined, long-term, in public institutions. Are we substituting one kind of neglect for another?

Lehman (1982) recently conducted an interesting study of quality of life issues and life satisfaction of 278 chronically ill residents of 30 large board and care homes in Los Angeles. Despite life conditions that would probably appear undesirable to the average American, over one-half of the residents said they were at least "mostly satisfied" in most areas of life. However, more than one-half of the residents were dissatisfied with their lives in three particular areas: finances, unemployment, and personal safety. One-third of the residents surveyed had been the victims of robberies and/or assaults in the previous year. The board and care home characteristic most correlated with satisfaction was privacy. These findings support the contention that supervised residential facilities may provide a reasonable alternative to hospitalization for many patients.

Richard Lamb (1979), in an article entitled "Roots of Neglect of the Long-term Mentally Ill," asks the crucial question, "How could professionals highly trained and skilled in the understanding of human behavior, and with a major responsibility for the fate of the mentally ill, be so insensitive to the needs their charges, not once but repeatedly?" (p. 201).

THE DETERMINANTS OF CHRONICITY

The Patient

Chronic patients are considered difficult to treat. Most of them belong to the lowest socioeconomic groups and are undereducated, unskilled, socially isolated, and in need of endless psychiatric care and public assistance. Often they come to treatment only when they face a crisis or an emergency and, even then, they do not come voluntarily but are often brought in by relatives, neighbors, or the police. They are more interested in survival than they are in self-realization or self-understanding. When psychotherapy is made available to them, a therapeutic alliance is difficult to establish. If such patients feel pressured in any way, it is common for incapacitating symptoms to develop, or for them to use their symptomatology in pseudopsychopathic ways in order to manipulate the therapist.

The Family

It is estimated that 70 percent of seriously ill mental patients have family members who can or will be involved with them after discharge from a hospital (Talbott 1983). The role of the family in the chronic patient's ability to survive in the community is now well recognized. Poor tolerance of patient symptoms, stress, and turmoil is directly related to early rehospitalization. Families tend to be most distressed by bizarre, intrusive, and agitated behavior with poor task functioning. Those who cope most effectively with their mentally ill relatives are characterized by greater acceptance, less intrusiveness, avoidance of rigid statements, a better ability to listen, lack of fear, and a positive attitude. In addition, the work of Vaughn and associates (1976) on "Expressed Emotion" of family members suggests a direct relationship between this variable and relapse in schizophrenia. The most favorable outcome has occurred in patients with low expressed emotion families, who have remained on maintenance drug therapy and have had only limited contact with family members (Brown et al. 1972). Hatfield (1983) notes that the success of the movement toward community care at this time depends to a large extent on the capacity of families to bear this great burden.

Another source of concern is the level of misunderstanding and distrust that is often reported between professionals and families. Family members find the characterizations and stereotypes of professionals to be inaccurate and damaging. More recently, these families have become active advocates and have formed a national organization, the National Alliance for the Mentally Ill (NAMI), with affiliated groups in most major U.S. cities.

The Mental Health Professionals

In contrast to most public sector patients, mental health professionals usually have middle class values and orientations. Their training is traditional, and is not geared to the treatment of lower income patients with chronic illnesses. Most care providers seek to derive personal and professional satisfaction from their work, and hope that their patients will show some change toward independent functioning, effective adaptation, and self-understanding. But when they frequently see chronic patients become arrested in a seemingly never-ending helpless and dependent relationship, they experience a sense of personal failure and inadequacy in their healing abilities, and instead seek patients who will reaffirm their sense of self-worth. This problem increases the tendency among mental health professionals (especially psychiatrists) to become more committed to the private sector—which usually treats patients that are not as ill—than to the public sector, which is burdened with the ongoing care of the chronic mentally ill.

Society and Social Class

Society places the fate of chronic patients in the hands of government. Elected officials and bureaucrats tend to make their decisions regarding the care of chronic patients on the basis of economic and political expedience rather than on research recommendations.

The general public continues to be afraid of madness and mental patients. In a classic work, "Closed Rank," Cumming and Cumming (1957) studied public attitudes toward mental illness in Canada, and found that people tried to deny the very existence of mental illness and tended to close ranks against the mentally ill. A replication of this study in the same town several years later revealed almost identical results. There has, however, been some recent evidence of a steadily increasing acceptance of the mentally ill, and an improvement in attitudes toward these patients, especially if they are able to assume "normal roles" in the community (Talbott 1983).

Hollingshead and Redlich (1983), in their study of relationships between social class and mental illness, found striking social class differences in the prevalence of psychosis. The occurrence of major mental illness was especially high in the lowest class. These investigators also found a disinclination by the therapists to treat patients from the lower socioeconomic classes, regardless of diagnosis.

ALTERNATIVE TREATMENT PROGRAMS

The needs of the chronic mental patient in the community are varied and numerous. They include drug therapy, case management, psychotherapy, family intervention, crisis intervention, low cost housing, financial support, employment or vocational rehabilitation, socialization, recreation, supervision, and advocacy. Meeting these needs adequately is, therefore, an overwhelming task for any single service provider. A comprehensive approach to addressing the complex and multiple needs of this special patient population requires the development of a complex service delivery system. Such a system must be well coordinated, and must include inpatient, outpatient, and emergency services, together with psychosocial programs; and it must provide financial, housing, social, recreational, and vocational rehabilitation services.

Continuity of care must be central to the delivery of mental health services. Unfortunately, this is more frequently a goal than a reality (Granet and Talbott 1978). There is no single approach to ensure continuity of care, because of the idiosyncrasies and biases of different agencies, and because of the problems of duplication and lack of coordination of services (Bachrach 1981). Although research in general has not been systematic, some principles governing the delivery of mental health services can be inferred. These include acceptance of the chronic patient, acknowledgement of his or her special needs, provision of a range of coordinated services, promotion of interagency communications to monitor progress, and the identification of flaws in mental health programs.

Psychosocial rehabilitation efforts are usually hampered by the problem of recidivism, especially in patients who are homeless, friendless, and with no available support systems. Many approaches have been tried throughout the years. Fairweather and associates (1960) studied a large group of chronic patients who were discharged into homes that were run by the patients themselves under minimal supervision. Others have found that it is possible to reduce recidivism in homeless and friendless patients if small residential systems of mutual support are utilized after discharge. In these settings, the disabilities of one patient are compensated for by the strengths of the other members of the group. Mutual help seems to strengthen their assets and minimize their liabilities.

Based on the favorable results that were obtained by the experience of Fountain House and Fellowship House, NIMH modestly funded several pilot projects that were called 'community support programs' (CSPs) in 1977. These psychosocial rehabilitation centers were developed to provide comprehensive support systems for adults with seriously disabling chronic mental illness, and specifically designed to address the needs of the deinstitutionalized chronic patient. It was recognized that mental health agencies were unable to meet all the supportive service needs of this target patient group. The programs usually had four basic components: 1. Socialization programs were developed by the patient-members themselves that included all day, evening, and weekend activities. 2. Vocational programs offered opportunities for the development of skills and attitudes that were more compatible with the work world. Transitional employment programs provided work opportunities by contractual agreements with public and private employers. 3. Residential programs with largely unsupervised apartment living arrangements was another component. At the federal level, the CSP initiative helped develop the HUD/HEW Demonstration programs, to provide financial support for purchase and rehabilitation of small, community based residences. In addition, rent subsidies were available through these programs for those persons considered eligible in the community. 4. Case management facilitated the patients' movement through the available resources.

During the Carter administration, NIMH and Congress undertook two policy initiatives based, at least in part, on the favorable experiences of CSP: NIMH's National Plan for the Chronically Mentally Disabled, and the Mental Health System Act, CP-L-96-398. However, during the Reagan administration, many of these program initiatives have been severely curtailed by cuts in funding, and the Mental Health Systems Act was repealed and replaced by the omnibus Budget Reconciliation Act. In addition, thousands of mentally disabled patients whose cases were reviewed by the Social Security Administration had their benefits terminated. More recently, due to an increasing and disproportionate number of mental patients affected by the review process, and because of pressure from professional groups, the Department of Health and Human Services has announced changes that will liberalize standards for disability determination and the exemption from review of two-thirds of all mental impairment cases (Morrisey and Goldman 1984).

CONCLUSIONS

The treatment of the severely and chronically mentally ill has alternated throughout history between therapies that have silenced, confined, and neglected them, and others that have voiced their concerns, liberated them from confinement, and forced their visibility in the streets and social agencies of our communities. The locus for care of these patients has been shifted from institution to community and back again with each cycle of reform and innovation (Morrisey and Goldman 1984). An analysis of this trend reveals a discernible pattern of neglect. On first examination, the roots of this pattern appear to be external: economic, social, professional, and political. However, it soon becomes apparent that unconscious thoughts, feelings, and attitudes about the chronically mentally ill have also contributed to the development and maintenance of a persistent ambivalence that permeates our dealings with the chronic mental patient.

It is well known today that psychiatrists, both in the private and public sectors, have been insufficiently involved in the direct treatment of chronic mental patients. This has resulted in a vacuum that has been filled by other mental health professionals and paraprofessionals. To remedy this problem several authors have suggested that medical education and psychiatric training programs be modified to stimulate interest in the care of chronic mental patients (Nielsen et al. 1981). Ideally, the teaching of medical students and the training of psychiatry residents should provide intense, useful contact with chronic patients, with faculty supervisors serving as role models committed to the treatment of such patients. Such an approach would ultimately provide the psychiatrist with the knowledge and skills that are required to perform an adequate assessment, and to formulate a comprehensive and coordinated treatment plan for these seriously disabled chronic patients.

References

Bachrach LC: Continuity of care for chronic mental patients: a conceptual analysis. Am J Psychiatry 138:1449-1456, 1981

Brown GW, Birley JL, Wing JL: Influences of family life and social factors in the course of psychiatric illness. Br J Psychiatry 129:241-258, 1972

Cumming E, Cumming J: Closed Ranks: An Experiment in Mental Health Education. Cambridge, Harvard University Press, 1957

Fairweather GW, Simon R, Gebhard ME, et al: Relative effectiveness of psychotherapeutics: a multicriteria comparison of four programs for three different patient groups. Psychological Monographs 429:1-25, 1960

Gralnick A: Deinstitutionalization: origins and signs of failure. American Journal of Social Psychiatry 3:8-12, 1983

Granet RB, Talbott JA: The continuity agent: creating a new role to bridge the gaps in the mental health system. Hosp Community Psychiatry 29:132-133, 1978

Hatfield A: What families want of family therapy, in Family in Schizophrenia. Edited by McFarland WR. New York, Guilford Press, 1983

Greenblatt M: Dynamics of institutional change: the future of the mental hospital. Journal of the Bronx State Hospital 1:89-99, 1973

Hollingshead AB, Redlich FC: Social Class and Mental Illness: A Community Study. New York, Wiley Publications, 1983

Jones M: Social Psychiatry in the Community, in Hospitals and in Prisons. Springfield, Illinois: Charles C Thomas, 1962

Lamb R: Roots of neglect of the long term mentally ill. Psychiatry 42:201-207, 1979

Lehman AF, Ward NC, Linn LS: Chronic mental patients: the quality of life issue. Am J Psychiatry 139:1271-1276, 1982

Morrisey JP, Goldman HH: Cycles of reform in the care of the chronically mentally ill. Hosp Community Psychiatry 35:785-793, 1984

Nielsen AC, Stein LI, Talbott JA: Encouraging psychiatrists to work with chronic patients. Hosp Community Psychiatry 32:767-775, 1981

Pepper B, Ryglewicz H: Testimony for the neglected: the mentally ill in the post deinstitutionalized age. Am J Orthopsychiatry 52 (3):388-392, 1982

Reich R: Care of the chronically mentally ill: a national disgrace. Am J Psychiatry 130:911-912, 1973

Talbott JA: Care of the chronically mentally ill still a national disgrace. Am J Psychiatry 136:688-689, 1979

Talbott JA: The chronic mental patient: what have we learned? American Journal of Social Psychiatry 3:37-42, 1983

Vaughn CE, Leff JP: The influence of family and social factors in the course of psychiatric illness. Br J Psychiatry 129:125-137, 1976

2

Public Policy and the Care of the Chronic Patient

Allan Beigel, M.D.

2

Public Policy and the Care of the Chronic Patient

The principal purpose of this chapter is to describe some of the major themes that will shape current and future policy with regard to the care of the chronic mentally ill patient. For reasons that this discussion will attempt to explain, this is a time of unusual fluidity within the general mental health care delivery system, a time of increased opportunity for either progress or regression. It is hoped that progress will be the result over the next several years, but the possibility for regression cannot be ignored.

Unusual and significant progress has been made during the past decade in public policy with regard to the care of the chronic mentally ill. However, it should be pointed out that this progress has not necessarily been a result of careful thinking on the part of a large number of policy makers, or of a carefully preconceived and brilliantly executed plan. Rather, this progress to a larger extent has been a consequence of the initiatives of a few selected individuals and groups who, acting out of their own intense interests in this area, have obtained the necessary public support that has gained attention for this underserved population. Their objectives have been assisted by several fortuitous events that focused greater attention on the plight of the chronic mentally ill. These events will now be discussed.

MILESTONES

A National Plan

The first milestone was the development of a National Plan for the Chronically Mentally Ill (1980), a process that began in the second half of the 1970s. The publication of this document, almost still-born in 1980 by the Carter Administration as it entered its last days, was less than dramatic. In fact, the Plan never received official approval and was released as an informational document in order to ensure that it did not stay on the shelf and become covered with dust. Nevertheless, it was important, because it provided a basis for later attention to the needs of the chronic mentally ill.

President's Commission on Mental Health

A concurrent portion of that Plan was provided by the Final Report of the President's Commission on Mental Health (1978), which identified the chronic mentally ill as one of four populations that was either unserved, underserved, or inappropriately served. The publication of this document, and the attendant process, provided the first opportunity for both policy makers and the general public to understand that the chronic mentally ill, along with patients who are either children, aged, or minorities, were special segments of the total mentally ill population whose needs were not being met successfully within the system at that time. There were some policy makers within government, both at the federal level and state levels, who had recognized this prior to the Final Report of the President's Commission; but this document, along with the National Plan for the Chronically Mentally Ill, brought this issue into greater focus for all policy makers and for the public at large.

Community Support Program

A third event that helped to shape public policy for the care of the chronic mentally ill was the initiation, originally within a demonstration framework, of the Community Support Program (CSP) by the National Institute of Mental Health (NIMH). This occurred in 1977, during the first year of the Carter Administration, as leaders at NIMH became aware that policies and initiatives were insufficient to provide an impetus for community mental health programs that would properly focus their resources on the chronic mentally ill. This realization emerged as APA data (Talbott, 1978) became available that clearly demonstrated that community mental health centers were treating the less serious mentally ill to a greater degree than they were treating the chronic mentally ill. This was not surprising, considering that the major focus of the community mental health center program during its initial decade, from 1963 to 1973, was to expand the accessibility and availability of services to all Americans through a wide variety of mechanisms. While this objective was achieved with great success, one of its by-products was the failure to provide adequate care to those special populations that came to be known at the time of the Carter Commission as the unserved, the underserved, or the inappropriately served. For the chronic mentally ill, the problems were exacerbated by the phenomenon of deinstitutionalization, which had led to the return of a fairly large number of chronic mentally ill persons to the community without the necessary initiatives and programs in the community to provide adequate support to meet their needs. As a result, the CSP became a demonstration vehicle for a series of programs. By focusing on the chronic mentally ill patient, this program provided an important public policy directive to all community mental health programs that received federal funds—they had to be more responsive to the needs of the chronic mentally ill.

Improvements in Housing

A derivative, but nonetheless important, event that occurred in relation to the initiatives of the CSP was the focus that emerged in the late 1970s and early 1980s on housing for the chronic mentally ill. The increasing recognition that appropriate and affordable housing for the chronic mentally ill person was a significant "therapeutic" component of effective care was important, because it emphasized that the needs of this population could only be met by a coordinated public policy effort that would embrace areas not traditionally presumed to be part of medical or health care. Consequently, although these housing initiatives were not completely successful, they signaled an understanding on the part of some policy makers that the problem of the chronic mentally ill person could not be approached from a public policy perspective, without recognizing that there were nonmedical issues that needed to be addressed.

The Block Grant Approach

When the Reagan Administration came into office in 1981, this administration stated that the focus of mental health initiatives should move to the state level from the federal level, regardless of the population to be served. This important public policy shift was designed ostensibly to merge responsibility with authority. These policy makers felt that the initiative that the federal government had been called upon to provide through the community mental health centers legislation of 1963 was no longer needed and, furthermore, that an over-involved federal government would simply deter the states from being able to act in a manner consistent with the responsibility they had always had. As a basis for this decision, many policy makers pointed to the fact that even during the height of federal involvement in community mental health center programming, the overwhelming percentage of dollars being spent on the care of all chronic mentally ill persons, like all other mentally ill persons, was being appropriated by the state. In 1981, all previously dispensed federal dollars were transferred to the state level, although in a smaller amount, for distribution. Thus, from a period of intense federal activity from a public policy perspective during the last half of the 1970s with regard to the care of the chronic mentally ill, the scene shifted very rapidly to the states during the first half of the 1980s. Whether the states will continue to be the focus of activity during the latter half of the 1980s remains open to question in view of some of the issues that will be raised later in this chapter.

With these events serving as a historical backdrop, we can now examine some of the more salient themes that will shape public policy regarding the care of the chronic mentally ill patient during the coming years.

THEMES FOR TODAY AND TOMORROW

While these major themes fall into several different categories, no category stands out as being more important than that of financing. Consequently, within this discussion, the major emphasis will be given to those themes that relate to financial issues. Other, nonfinancial, themes will be touched upon briefly. The brief discussion of these other themes is not intended to signal any lack of recognition of their importance, but simply to underscore that in the current era of fiscal constraint, financial themes will probably be the most dominant area of concern to public policy makers.

Targeted versus Non-Targeted Financing

The recognition during the early and mid-1970s that significant components of the mentally ill population were unserved, underserved, or inappropriately served through a generic approach to financing has led to the development and implementation of a more "targeted" approach to financing of mental health care. The CSP, with its limited funding, was a federal expression of this approach. It remains, despite the best efforts of the Reagan administration, the one area of direct federal support for mental health services that is not within the block grant program.

Ironically, the actions of Congress that have served to preserve and protect the funding for the CSP have been mirrored by similar "targeted" approaches at the state level. For example, in Arizona, legislation during the past five years has created a separate stream of funding for the care of the chronic mentally ill. Furthermore, in the Arizona state legislature a recent proposal for the reorganization of mental health services stipulated that funding from the state be distributed according to a set formula to local administrative agencies, allowing these agencies to determine the way these resources should be spent. It is interesting that the current proposal restricts those funds distributed to local agencies to "generic" funding, and prohibits the distribution of funds that have been made available for this special purpose of caring for the chronic mentally ill. These funds would be retained by the state for direct appropriation to programs that meet the objectives of the legislation.

These events, taken together, seem to suggest a recognition on the part of some public policy makers that the needs of unserved and underserved populations, such as the chronic mentally ill, never will be met successfully unless funds are targeted for programs that address their needs. Without questioning the good intentions of providers, there appears to be an emerging belief that unless protected funding status for the chronic mentally ill is maintained, the natural chain of events will be to deemphasize programs for this population in the service system. To the extent that a targeted approach to funding of the care of the chronic mentally ill is eliminated, one can anticipate, based on past experience, that services for that population will decrease in coming years.

Traditional Reimbursement Approaches

One of the reasons that targeted funding for the chronic mentally ill has been important in meeting the needs of this population has been the failure of traditional reimbursement approaches to address those same needs. This failure has been a result of two important problems. First, traditional reimbursement approaches tend to emphasize acute inpatient and outpatient care. These represent two ends of the service spectrum which, when one considers the needs of the chronic mental patient, are an incomplete portion of the system of services that this population requires. Second, since many chronic mentally ill persons are individuals who have fallen by the wayside, they are usually not covered by the traditional reimbursement programs available through employers and government. As a result, their needs are met only if public financing is available and if that financing is, as indicated earlier, targeted to meet their needs. At the same time, however, it is important to recognize that traditional approaches to reimbursement are changing; government and third party payers are looking for new ways to achieve cost containment, without having to resort to the open-ended, price related reimbursement system that has been so costly.

The pre-paid system of care is an alternative to traditional reimbursement approaches. This system takes a per capita approach to a specific population, and has two advantages for the care of the chronic mentally ill person. First, the pre-paid system could transcend the barrier created by more traditional approaches that focus only on providing reimbursement for certain kinds of services. The pre-paid system would examine the needs of the population in question, design the service system that would meet those needs, determine what its cost would be, and ration that cost on a per capita basis throughout the designated population. Second, this approach would help to move beyond the barriers that are often created by a reimbursement system dominated by concerns as to which providers are eligible for reimbursement. In this pre-paid system, the emphasis would be on the quality of services and on the development of a system to deliver those services—involving all types of providers appropriately placed within the system—to do the job that they have best been trained to do. This approach could, therefore, foster a more cooperative partnership among mental health providers in the interest of reducing costs and meeting the needs of a large population of individuals to be served.

The strength of this approach, however, is also its potential weakness: In order to keep costs down, policy makers may attempt to screen out individuals such as the chronic mentally ill, who require more intense forms of care. In the long run, this would be disadvantageous, because it would simply shift the burden of care for these individuals to another system of financing which, in turn, would have to pay for that care at a later date and at a higher total cost.

Prospective Payment

The advent of prospective payment has stirred considerable controversy. Mental health care has been excluded from the prospective payment system at the outset, providing a unique opportunity to force psychiatrists and other mental health providers to determine how this approach to financing can be structured in a way that best meets the needs of the population it is designed to serve.

To achieve a positive result for the chronic mentally ill population from the introduction of prospective payment, two problems will have to be addressed. The first problem is the current, unnecessarily rigid, approach of the Diagnosis Related Groupings (DRGs). As now conceptualized, they do not take into account several factors that are particularly relevant to psychiatric patients and, more importantly, to the needs of chronic mentally ill patients. The first factor is the severity of illness; the second is the level of disability. Without taking into consideration these two factors, any DRG approach for psychiatric patients will tend to favor the treatment of the more acutely ill individual, whose ability to recover from a mental disorder is greater than that of the chronic mentally ill person. If these problems are to be overcome, psychiatrists and other researchers must further refine our diagnostic groupings in order to ensure that they are as homogeneous as possible so that proper fiscal planning can take place.

The second problem that must be addressed is the current limitation of prospective payment to inpatient care. Inpatient care is certainly the most costly, and often least productive, form of intervention for the chronic mentally ill person. As long as prospective payment systems focus on inpatient care, the tendency will be to force chronic mentally ill patients prematurely out of inpatient settings and into other settings where services may not be available or payment for them affordable. A prospective payment approach would be most successful for chronic mentally ill persons if it is implemented along the entire spectrum of care, and not solely on inpatient care.

Health Care versus Social Care

While some progress has been made in recognizing and addressing the multiple needs of chronic mentally ill persons, the way in which the diverse needs of this population can be brought together in a single financing system has not been found.

All too often it is the tendency of policy makers to try to shift the burden of responsibility for the care of this population, and the funding of services for it, to either the "social" or to the "health care" end of the spectrum. However, when both ends of the spectrum are under fiscal constraints (resulting in initiatives designed to foster either health care cost containment or social disability cost containment) the outcome for the chronic mentally ill person can only be negative.

No situation could be more tragic for the chronic mentally ill patient than the specter of a government that attempts to cut off disability support for that population, while at the same time denying them access to services through more stringent health care reimbursement mechanisms. The Catch-22 aspects of this situation are alarming because they result in pitting policy makers, with responsibility for cost containment in each of the two major areas of care, against each other.

In this regard, one wonders whether it will ever be possible for government and other policy makers to recognize that the design of any system of care (including its financing) for a specific population must begin with a careful assessment of the needs of that population, rather than with bureaucratic paradigms that determine allocation of resources.

Successful financing of the care of the chronic mentally ill requires a "bottoms up" approach to financial planning from the perspective of the needs of the population at risk. Since those needs are both medical and social in nature, cooperation among policy makers in both arenas is essential. Without this, success in planning an approach to the care and treatment of this population is doubtful.

Before concluding this discussion, there are two additional, nonfinancial, public policy issues that deserve mention, since they will also influence the future course of public policy regarding the care of the chronic mentally ill patient. While neither is financial in nature, both have the potential for having significant impact on approaches to financing.

Advances in Psychopharmacology

Recent advances in psychopharmacology have led practitioners, particularly psychiatrists, to have a greater armamentarium of therapeutic regimens available to assist in symptom reduction than ever before. This will enable more chronic mentally ill patients to remain in a behavioral and mental state that is, at least, consistent with community placement. As advances in psychopharmacology and other therapeutic techniques continue, there will be an increasing burden on public policy makers to design non-inpatient oriented service resources for chronic mentally ill patients, and to assure that appropriate funding for them is present. Without these changes, the full potential of the advances in psychopharmacology will not be realized. The proper service resources and funding must be put into place if the results of psychopharmacological advances—the enabling of the chronic mental patient to live in the community—are to be positive.

The Role of the Consumer

The role of the consumer movement on behalf of the chronic mentally ill patient has changed considerably over the past decade. The antipsychiatric and antiprofessional orientation of much of this movement during the late 1970s and early 1980s appears to be diminishing. A new consumer based movement has emerged that emphasizes a partnership between the families of chronic mentally ill patients and professionals in the pursuit of reallocation of scarce resources to meet the needs of this population.

It is fortunate that this new alliance has emerged in this time of fiscal constraint, since it probably offers the best hope for focusing public policy makers on the essence of the problems that exist and that must be solved before the needs of this population can be adequately addressed. It therefore behooves all professionals to work closely with these consumer groups; their support for professionally directed services is essential if the needs of the chronic mentally ill population are to be met.

SUMMARY

It is clear that we have reached a critical juncture in the development of public policy with regard to the care of the chronic mental patient. At no time since the end of World War II has more public attention been focused on the needs of this population. This has resulted from a combination of factors, including the consequences of the deinstitutionalization movement of the 1960s and 1970s, the compelling stories of the homeless during the last several years as aggravated by economic conditions, and the problems that have emerged from the impact of rising health care costs.

All of these factors, operating together, have created an environment in which a unique opportunity exists to address the needs of a population that has now been recognized as special. What is long overdue for this special population is a sane and thoughtful approach to public policy formulation.

References

President's Commission on Mental Health: Final Report, Washington, D.C., U.S. Government Printing Office, 1978

Talbott JA: The Chronic Mental Patient: Problems, Solutions, and Recommendations for Public Policy. Washington, D.C., American Psychiatric Association, 1978

Toward a National Plan for the Chronically Mentally Ill. Washington, D.C., U.S. Department of Health and Human Services, 1980

3

The Chronic Young Adult: Trends in Deinstitutionalization and Public Sector Hospital Care

Richard J. Carlson, M.D.
Pedro Ruiz, M.D.

3

The Chronic Young Adult: Trends in Deinstitutionalization and Public Sector Hospital Care

Over the last several years there has been a dramatic increase in the population of young adult chronic psychiatric patients, occurring while patients are being released from state and county hospitals in large numbers in the continuing process of deinstitutionalization. Most of these younger patients have not had long stays in an institution. Others have never been admitted to a psychiatric hospital. Therefore, most of these young adult patients could not be labeled as institutionalized. Nevertheless, they have developed degrees of chronicity of their illnesses that require psychiatric and social care. The availability of long-term treatment facilities has been diminishing, but the requirement of hospital treatment for chronic patients, both younger and older, has not diminished. The burden of hospitalization rests upon the public mental hospital facilities; that is, inpatient units of general hospitals, local psychiatric hospitals, and the county and state hospital systems. At the same time, outpatient treatment settings and Community Support Programs (CSPs) have had to expand in order to meet these patients' needs for their long-term care.

Critics of the deinstitutionalization movement have pointed out some of the inadequacies of community treatment facilities in handling the needs of these patients who are dependent upon so many social and medical networks for the treatment of their chronic illnesses, and even for their day-to-day needs and survival, in some cases. Homeless people living in the streets may include a large number of chronic patients (Prevost 1982). Institutional care, with the ability to provide asylum, is considered necessary in many instances (Bachrach 1984). Starting as far back as 1955, proponents of the release of patients from the mental institutions had hoped that chronicity of illness would become less of a problem; but chronicity has continued in spite of deinstitutionalization. Nevertheless, the momentum has continued in the direction away from hospitalization and toward community support and outpatient treatment. Problems arise, however, when patients require inpatient services in the public sector, either on a short-term or on a long-term basis.

THE YOUNG ADULT CHRONIC PATIENT

As a group, young adult chronic psychiatric patients have visibly emerged over the last several years. They have assumed increasing prominence by their sheer numbers, as well as by their use of psychiatric services. They fall into the 18- to 35-year-old age group, and their presence appears to be a consequence of deinstitutionalization and population trends (Bachrach 1982). Although some of these patients have been hospitalized and released, most of them represent a group of patients who were never institutionalized, but who, in the past, would have been. In addition, most of them belong to the "baby boom" cohort, which now accounts for approximately one-third of the U.S. population. Although the rate of mental illness is not unusual, the absolute numbers are considerably higher than they are for other age cohorts. These young adult patients have a variety of disorders, but are predominately schizophrenic. Indeed, Pepper and associates (1981) studied this group of patients and found that almost 60 percent have schizophrenia. Major affective disorders accounted for about seven percent of the patients in their study; borderline and other personality disorders accounted for approximately 12 percent; and organic mental disorders and mental retardation together accounted for about 11 percent. Slightly more than one-half of this population are males. They are consumers of outpatient, emergency, and brief-stay public hospital services.

Chronicity of their psychiatric disorders has been defined by Minkoff (1979) using three parameters: the psychiatric diagnosis, the level of disability, and duration of illness. In terms of diagnosis, there is general agreement that disorders such as schizophrenia, major affective disorders, and organic brain syndromes, as well as other psychoses, tend to predominate. Disability may result from limitations in three or more of the following areas: self-care, receptive and expressive language, learning, mobility, self-direction, capacity for independent living, and economic self-sufficiency. Duration of illness as defined by hospitalization is difficult to measure. Most patients are hospitalized for less than 90 days in state hospitals. The CSP of the National Institute of Mental Health (NIMH) specified that a single hospitalization for at least six months during the last five years, or five or more hospitalizations within a 12 month period, was sufficient to be labeled severely mentally disabled. As patients spend less and less time in institutional settings, the duration aspect of chronicity may have to be redefined.

Peele and Palmer (1980) have used six operational criteria in identifying chronicity: patient's deficit in functioning and/or responsiveness to treatment; presence of dependent lifestyle; psychiatric diagnosis; amount of time spent in psychiatric hospitals; legal eligibility for financial entitlements; and indefinite need for supportive services.

It is estimated by Goldman and colleagues (1981) that there are at least two million chronic mental patients in the United States. Close to one-half of them are in institutions, but the overwhelming majority of them are in nursing home facilities with diagnoses of senility and other chronic mental disorders.

Special Characteristics and Needs of These Patients

Regardless of their symptom profiles, Pepper (1981) found that chronic young adult patients shared two characteristics: their severe difficulties in social functioning, and their tendency to use mental health services inappropriately. This is a highly mobile group of individuals, traveling from place to place, slipping in and out of treatment, frequently noncompliant, aggressive and intolerant of frustration, and having difficulty establishing therapeutic relationships (Bachrach 1982). Schwartz and Goldfinger (1981) found that they tend to alienate the sources of support in their lives, such as family, friends, and significant others. Gruenberg (1967) described the "social breakdown syndrome," in which patients who are institutionalized are characterized by negativism, apathy, and poor social and psychological functioning. Since most of the young adult chronic patients have never been institutionalized, the prevalence of this syndrome among them appears to be a reflection of their illness rather than a reflection of their treatment. Many of these patients have become involved in criminal activities, and in one study (Caton 1981), a little more than 20 percent of the chronic schizophrenics followed during the study year had committed crimes.

These patients tend to use public sector outpatient and inpatient facilities, with little discrimination for the appropriateness of the services used (Schwartz 1981). When in crisis, as they frequently are, they may utilize crisis intervention services and community mental health services for social and psychiatric needs. Often they do not seek treatment for themselves, but are brought to the hospital on an involuntary basis. Following hospitalization, they frequently do not comply with further treatment and, as a result, the whole cycle begins again.

In short, these patients tend to be part of the "revolving door" syndrome, in which they are admitted and discharged rapidly, only to be readmitted to one hospital or another. Prior to deinstitutionalization, relatively homogeneous services could be provided to a population of patients who required hospitalization. Young adult chronic mental patients have varying histories of hospital treatment, various needs, and erratic histories of outpatient followup, so that treatment planning with this group of patients is extremely difficult. Robbins and colleagues (1978) have described them as being "in a state of disequilibrium," indicating that these patients cannot adapt to the community, and they cannot remain in the hospital. Robbins and associates have also emphasized difficulties in providing adequate treatment if they remain in the hospital for only a short period of time and do not participate in treatment in the community. Bachrach (1982) has emphasized the diversity of the service agencies that provide care in the public sector, which results in a fragmentation of service delivery. Patients frequently, in addition to being unable to look after some basic day-to-day needs, have not found the resources to admit themselves into a system of care and then follow through with it. The psychiatric care systems have been criticized for not being able to provide adequate facilities for continuing treatment of these young adult chronic patients, who Segal (1980) has described as "the most difficult mental patients of the 1980s."

Sheets and associates (1982) have hypothesized three subgroups of young adult chronic psychiatric patients. They describe the first group as the high-functioning group, felt to do better while in remission and to demand less energy of the treatment center. Individuals in this group are usually of a higher socioeconomic status and are relatively new to the mental health system. Some of them may actively participate in their treatment, thereby making provision of services easier. They probably blend into the general population and may not be easily identified as chronic mental patients. Another group, called the low-energy, low-demand group, consists of chronic patients who probably entered the mental health system at a young age and appear to be burned out early. They are passive and poorly motivated, and do not do well even in remission. They are deeply enmeshed in the treatment system and in their role as patients. They usually accept mental health services and are, therefore, relatively easy to manage. The third group, described as the high-energy, high-demand group, is the one that seems to generate most of the difficulties in the delivery of services. They are exceedingly mobile, have fluctuating functional abilities, and make many demands from social and mental health facilities. They have low frustration tolerance, frequent acting out, and encounters with the law. Because they do not adhere to treatment, they are usually involved in "revolving door" situations. By dividing young adult patients into these three subgroups, the authors have attempted to show variations in the composition of this recently emerging group of chronic psychiatric patients. This can be of assistance in individualizing treatment programs, and in allocating resources based upon particular needs and motivations of the patient.

THE EFFECTS OF DEINSTITUTIONALIZATION

Deinstitutionalization of public mental hospitals has had a serious impact, not only on younger chronic psychiatric patients, but on all chronic patients who have required hospital care. The outpatient facilities in the public sector are usually less than adequate to meet the myriad needs of these patients. The deinstitutionalization movement has attempted to avoid long-term hospital stays, while at the same time promoting the growth of outpatient facilities in community settings.

As early as 1955, state hospitals began a decline in the number of resident patients: from 559,000 to 191,000 in 1975, a two-thirds decrease (Platman 1983). The results are that fewer of the chronic mentally ill are being admitted to or are remaining in institutions on a long-term basis. James Prevost (1982), Commissioner of the New York State Office of Mental Health, has pointed out that there is a need to understand the impact that these patients have on the community in general. He has emphasized the aspects of criminal activity and street life that these patients experience.

Bachrach (1983a) lists five major areas of concern in the provision of services to deinstitutionalized patients: *1.* those with chronic mental disorders have a great range of disabilities and service needs that usually span the course of a lifetime, but the planning of services has been geared toward single-episode usage; 2. the most severely impaired patients may not be able to use these services well because they tend to be oriented to patients who are motivated and can change; 3. the stigma of the treatment of the chronic mentally ill is still prominent in community based treatment services; 4. quality of care is reduced, due to fragmentation among the agencies providing services; 5. semantic confusion in deinstitutionalization programs contributes to service delivery problems.

Over the last 30 years, the number of patients in mental institutions has continued to decline. However good the intentions of deinstitutionalization planners may have originally been, commentaries about the negative or harmful aspects of deinstitutionalization abound. These patients are achieving greater importance and visibility in the community as their numbers increase. Jones (1983) points to deinstitutionalization as the leading cause of the homeless living on the city streets. The homeless require shelter and the use of multiple social services for their basic needs. Frequently, the only services that they want are those of a hospital. They may either make attempts to be readmitted to the state hospital system, or they may inappropriately use facilities of local public hospitals, which have been oriented to acute care and short-term stay.

Gralnick (1983), writing in *The American Journal of Social Psychiatry,* reflects the views of many mental health experts by strongly stating that "there is mounting evidence of an enormous and growing group of chronic young adult patients in the community who have had little if any hospital care. They are major social and treatment problems, and are very refractory to the modalities we have available for them. The plight of most of our mentally ill in the community is desperate, if not downright shameful. Unsatisfactory as their care may have been in the state hospitals of the past, the patients received more professional and personal attention than patients today receive in the community. It is probably true that the economic costs are greater than ever, though hidden and diverted into other service areas."

Bachrach (1984) has recently commented on one of the classic functions of the state hospital, namely asylum. She emphasizes the function of institutions in providing residential care, medical services, relief to families, socialization for the patient, and the role of advocate for the chronic mentally ill patient.

ISSUES IN HOSPITAL CARE

As methods of treatment for the young adult chronic patient have changed over the years, with increasing importance being attached to outpatient management in the community, the requirement for psychiatric inpatient treatment has by no means been reduced (Caton 1982). Caton points out that episodes of rehospitalization are becoming the pattern. Young adult chronic patients are pervasive users of short-term public hospital services. They remain noninstitionalized, but frequently require the use of hospital services. Chronic young adults are not easily managed in an outpatient setting, and many are not well suited to treatment on an outpatient basis (Bachrach 1983b). Schwartz (1981) comments upon the difficulties involved in the inpatient management of the new young adult chronic patient. He emphasizes this patient's tendency to feel overwhelmed by the interpersonal interactions of an inpatient environment. Legal measures to keep the patient in the hospital may not work, because the patient may pull himself together adequately enough to be seen as harmless. The young adult chronic patient is also resistant to participation in group therapy and activity programs. Inpatient staff frequently feel frustrated because of his behavior, and there is a tendency toward rapid treatment and quick discharge. The chronic patient then returns either to the same hospital or to another facility.

Platman and colleagues (1983) found a "new" population of long-term patients in the Maryland public mental health system. The 18- to 34-year-old age group replaced the 35- to 64-year-old age group as the major admission cohort. Patients in the age range of 18 to 34 accounted for almost 20 percent of the long-term chronic mentally ill patients in the Wisconsin Community Support Program (Wagner 1981). Clearly, this group of young adult mental patients with a chronic psychiatric illness is a major consumer of inpatient services.

Herz and associates (1977) found that short-term inpatient treatment of 11 days was effective in the treatment of chronic schizophrenic patients. They pointed out cost effectiveness, improved social functioning, and no higher rate in standard readmission hospitalization. Longer stays, however, may be required for adequate discharge planning in certain cases. Caton (1982) found that length of inpatient stay bore no particular relationship to subsequent hospitalization, treatment compliance, or clinical or social functioning in a group of chronic schizophrenic patients.

The trend toward brief hospitalization continues, not only for economic reasons, but because many patients can be returned to the community after a short hospitalization. Approximately 80 percent of all patients admitted to state and county hospitals are discharged in less than 90 days (Goldman 1981). Dyck (1974) concurs, and comments that short-term hospitalization of less than two weeks is often all that is needed to allow some chronic patients to return to less expensive treatment settings. He emphasizes the need for a continuity of services to allow those transfers to occur. Kibel (1978) points out the usefulness of short-term hospitalization with structured environments in the treatment of young adult chronic patients, with particular emphasis on those with borderline personalities.

There appears to be a general consensus with regard to the broad characteristics of inpatient care for this special group. Of necessity, most young adult chronic patients are admitted to public sector hospitals for periods of less than one month. Often, due to their chronicity and diversity of needs, they are readmitted again and again because of their failure to cope in the community. Brief hospitalization is used for these patients in the 1980s, as opposed to the longer institutional stays of 20 or 30 years ago.

In the authors' experience, there are two important factors in the effective management of the young chronic patient in the short-term public hospital: continuity of care services and discharge planning. Continuity of care requires the smooth planning and integration of services on various levels, including state and county hospitals, public sector general hospitals, and the community facilities and outpatient treatment centers to which these patients are referred. Appropriate discharge planning is of paramount importance. Caton (1982), in a study of chronic schizophrenics, pointed out that subsequent hospitalizations bear a greater relation to the nature of the aftercare treatment provided and features of the patient's community environment, than they do to the actual length of inpatient stay. Herz and colleagues (1977) suggested that longer hospital stays may be necessary in some instances in order to devise adequate discharge plans for those patients who are without families.

We have found that specialized programs for the management

of chronic young adult patients are useful during the early phases of inpatient treatment. Rapid and effective treatment methods, development of positive and optimistic approaches to the younger chronic patient, and emphasis on family, social, community, and aftercare support systems are all valuable in the management and reintegration of the patient. Family meetings, where possible, should begin shortly after admission. These sessions are useful in formulating appropriate plans for discharge. Actual discharge planning should begin at the start of hospitalization and should emphasize three important components: appropriate plans for outpatient followup, which include medication maintenance and other necessary therapies; investigation of the patient's living situation, with arrangements for discharge to family, residential treatment center, halfway house, or other adequate facility; and a review of the patient's general financial and working situation, with necessary referral to the welfare department, disability determination agency, job training program, or any other appropriate agency. Following these pathways, the authors attempt to prevent relapse and readmission, and to diminish continuing chronic disabilities as much as possible during short inpatient stays.

FUTURE TRENDS

The process of deinstitutionalization, begun 30 years ago, continues to accelerate. Funding agencies, such as state or county governments, find it financially preferable to treat patients on an outpatient basis. The fact that it costs more to treat someone in a hospital setting is a reality with which we must live. Patients will continue to be discharged from the state hospitals, and fewer beds will be available for admission in the future. In consequence, the spotlight has been on the outpatient and residential facilities required for young adult chronic patients.

As we have seen, this population is a difficult one to treat for numerous reasons and, therefore, treatment programs must be well-coordinated and designed to meet the needs of these patients. Bachrach (1983b) lists the following components of an ideal service system: basic screening and referral services to objectively assess patients' needs; 24-hour crisis services to meet their acute needs; a network of residential alternatives, such as independent residences, halfway houses, group residences, cooperative apartments, lodge programs, foster care homes, nursing homes, board-and-care homes, and hotels; options in treatment settings that include partial hospitalization and inpatient care, either temporary or long-term; a range of treatment services consisting of social, recreational, vocational, employment, educational, physical, and psychotherapeutic modalities; transportation services to meet the specific needs of some patients; and information and evaluation services that examine patients' needs, program effectiveness, and the overall impact of the system in meeting the needs of the young chronic patient.

The development of the CSPs and the community mental health center system of NIMH has been viewed by some authors (Morrissey and Goldman 1984) as the newest cycle of institutional reform for the treatment of the chronic mentally ill. This approach offers care and rehabilitation through a system of support services in the community, rather than in a single institution. These authors speak of a process of "trans-institutionalization," in which patients are housed in community institutional settings such as those suggested by Bachrach (1983b) as being suitable residential alternatives to hospital placement. The CSPs have continued to receive limited funds from NIMH. It appears likely that emphasis on CSPs will continue, and that their services will have to expand to meet the needs of young adult chronic patients.

Some basic planning principles outlined by Bachrach (1984) are useful in the development of effective programs. These are: functional equivalence, cultural relevance, and trading-off of services. Functional equivalence refers to a variety of services sometimes meeting the same needs, such as the public hospital, halfway house, or boarding home, all of which provide residential care appropriate to a particular patient's needs. Communities have developed various types of residences and, for instance, where a state hospital may not be able to provide the necessary protection or care, another type of living situation may be appropriate. Cultural relevance applies to specific service systems in a particular community. The types of patients in a community, as well as community characteristics, may determine what types of service systems are developed. Potential trade-offs refer to certain services in the community being able to provide the necessary requirements and, therefore, making other types of care unnecessary.

Even with efforts directed at treatment and rehabilitation of young adult chronic patients in a variety of community settings, many of them continue to require long-term hospitalization. Sheets and associates (1982) express concern about those young adult chronic patients who just cannot function or respond to acute care models of service. Shore and Shapiro (1979) discuss a group of chronic mentally ill patients who have remained in the hospital despite deinstitutionalization. Young chronic patients are usually not a part of that particular group but, as we are learning, many of them do require institutional care. Frequently, types of institutional care provided in the community, such as supervised residences, halfway houses, and nursing home facilities are not adequate to meet the diverse needs of this population of young adult chronic patients. Sheets and associates (1982) emphasize the need for indefinite-term inpatient and community residential facilities for those patients who require them.

Bachrach (1984) reviews the functions of the mental hospital in the care of chronic patients. These include the provision of residential care, comprehensive medical services, relief to overburdened families, provision of a social network for the patient, and advocacy for the patient in obtaining goods and services. The author points out that community-based programs may not be able to provide these services, because some patients continue to require asylum, safety, and security, as well as other basic needs. There is a trend in recognizing that many chronic young adult patients require institutional care, and that community residential facilities and treatment programs may not be adequate in providing the necessary level of care required.

SUMMARY

There are several suggestions for future directions in the problematic care of the young adult chronic psychiatric patient. Community and outpatient programs must be optimally developed to serve those younger chronic patients who can adequately function outside of the hospital. Such patients must be guided to utilize social and psychiatric agencies to their benefit and to be rehabilitated to some levels of functioning. It is hoped that chronicity can be altered, or prevented, where possible. Brief-stay public sector inpatient facilities should be expanded to meet the treatment needs of this group of patients when they require immediate and rapid intervention. From this type of facility they can either quickly be returned to the community at an adequate level of functioning, or be transferred to a state hospital facility for continuing care. Finally, the integration and coordination of these services at local, county, and state levels is necessary for the proper functioning of the entire system.

References

Bachrach LL: Young adult chronic patients: an analytical review of the literature. Hosp Community Psychiatry 33:189-197, 1982

Bachrach LL: Concepts and issues in deinstitutionalization, in The Chronic Psychiatric Patient in the Community: Principles of Treatment. Edited by Barofsky I, Budson RD. New York, Spectrum Publications, 1983a

Bachrach LL: Planning services for the young adult schizophrenic outpatient. The Schizophrenic Outpatient (DuPont Pharmaceuticals) 2:1-12, 1983b

Bachrach LL: Asylum and chronically ill psychiatric patients. Am J Psychiatry 141:975-978, 1984

Caton CLM: The new chronic patient and the system of community care. Hosp Community Psychiatry 32:475-478, 1981

Caton CLM: Effect of length of inpatient treatment for chronic schizophrenics. Am J Psychiatry 139:856-861, 1982

Dyck G: The effect of a community mental health center upon state hospital utilization. Am J Psychiatry 131:453-456, 1974

Goldman HH, Gattozzi AA, Taube CA: Defining and counting the chronically mentally ill. Hosp Community Psychiatry 32:21-27, 1981

Gralnick A: Deinstitutionalization: origins and signs of failure. American Journal of Social Psychiatry 3:9-12, 1983

Gruenberg EM: The social breakdown syndrome: some origins. Am J Psychiatry 123:1481-1489, 1967

Herz MI, Endicott J, Spitzer RL: Brief hospitalization: a two-year follow-up. Am J Psychiatry 134:502-507, 1977

Jones RE: Street people and psychiatry: an introduction. Hosp Community Psychiatry 34:807-811, 1983

Kibel HD: The rationale for the use of group psychotherapy for borderline patients on a short-term unit. Int J Group Psychother 28:339-358, 1978

Minkoff K: A map of chronic mental patients, in The Chronic Mental Patient. Edited by Talbott JA. Washington, D.C., American Psychiatric Association, 1979

Morrissey JP, Goldman HH: Cycles of reform in the care of the chronically mentally ill. Hosp Community Psychiatry 35:785-793, 1984

Peele R, Palmer RR: Patient rights and patient chronicity. J Psychiatry and Law 59-71, 1980

Pepper B, Kirshner MC, Ryglewicz H: The young adult chronic patient: overview of a population. Hosp Community Psychiatry 32:463-469, 1981

Platman SR, Karahasan A, Booker TC: The new long-term patient in the public mental hospital. Am J Psychiatry 140:606-608, 1983

Prevost JA: Youthful chronicity: paradox of the 80s. Hosp Community Psychiatry 33:173, 1982

Robbins E, Stern M, Robbins L, et al: Unwelcome patients: where can they find asylum? Hosp Community Psychiatry 29:44-46, 1978

Schwartz SR, Goldfinger SM: The new chronic patient: clinical characteristics of an emerging subgroup. Hosp Community Psychiatry 32:470-474, 1981

Segal SP, Baumohl J: Engaging the disengaged: proposals on madness and vagrancy. Social Work 25:358-365, 1980

Sheets JL, Prevost J, Reihman J: Young adult chronic patients: three hypothesized subgroups. Hosp Community Psychiatry 33:197-203, 1982

Shore MF, Shapiro R: The effect of deinstitutionalization on the state hospital. Hosp Community Psychiatry 30:605-608, 1979

Wagner BA: Progress Report: Community Support Programs for the Long-Term Mentally Ill in Wisconsin. Madison, WI, Wisconsin Bureau of Mental Health, 1981

4

Polypharmacy in the Public Sector Care of Ambulatory Chronic Patients

George L. Adams, M.D.
Rosalind J. Dworkin, Ph.D.
Daryl K. Knox, M.D.

4

Polypharmacy in the Public Sector Care of Ambulatory Chronic Patients

Pharmacotherapy is an important component in the treatment of the chronic patient who is cared for in public sector mental health clinics. Treatment of the chronic patient implies care over an extended period of time. This extended time frame for maintenance of pharmacotherapy raises the issues of polypharmacy, over-medication, under-medication, as well as consequences of misdiagnosis. There is greater opportunity for patterns of prescribing to deviate from established guidelines of appropriate treatment, and these deviations may raise questions concerning the psychotherapeutic expertise of the psychiatrist, or the practicality of the guidelines. Moreover, there is increased opportunity for some differences in the patient population, such as gender, age, or ethnicity, to affect physician prescribing behavior. Prescribing must be viewed as a dynamic phenomenon. That is, one must be concerned about the longitudinal trends in medication use.

Unfortunately, most studies of prescribing issues, such as polypharmacy, have been done using cross-sectional designs. Estimates from such studies of the prevalence of polypharmacy vary considerably, depending upon the research site and the definition of polypharmacy used. Odejide (1980) documents a polypharmacy rate of 63 percent in an outpatient clinic in Nigeria. For that study, polypharmacy was defined as the addition of any other drug, including anticonvulsant and antiparkinsonian drugs. Similarly, using the same broad definition, Hemminki's (1977) work in Helsinki found a polypharmacy rate of 61 percent.

Studies done in the United States tend to define polypharmacy more narrowly, and also to find lower rates. Mason and colleagues' (1977) study of inpatients found that 30 percent of the prescriptions written were for two antipsychotics to be given together. At the other extreme, Baldessarini's (1984) study of inpatient medication found only 3.6 percent of the patients receiving two neuroleptics concurrently.

Studies of chronic patients using a more longitudinal approach are not plentiful (Laska et al. 1981). Diamond and associates (1976) did document changes in the patterns of pharmacotherapy over an 18-month period. They found a reduction in polypharmacy during that time. However, these changes were attributed to a series of peer review and intervention seminars in psychopharmacology. What the "normal" course of polypharmacy might be cannot be ascertained from this study. Laska and colleagues (1981) also noted changes in prescribing habits between 1972 and 1980. However, since each period used a different sample, the results are of limited utility.

The purpose of this paper is to examine the longitudinal trends in prescribing practices for chronic patients in an outpatient environment. Particular attention will focus upon issues of polypharmacy, especially with regard to antipsychotics. Among the questions addressed will be: *1.* What is the extent of polypharmacy, using both a broad and a narrow definition? 2. What are the changes in the patterns of prescribing over time? 3. How are the patterns related to diagnosis, years of treatment, gender, and ethnicity of the patient?

METHOD

This is a preliminary report of a longitudinal study of patients in five public sector community mental health ambulatory care clinics. The clinics are directed by the Community and Social Psychiatry Programs of the Baylor College of Medicine in Houston, Texas, for the Mental Health-Mental Retardation Authority (MHMRA) of Harris County, the locus of one of the largest public mental health care networks in the United States. The clinics serve mostly seriously ill, chronic patients.

In March, 1983, data were collected from the charts of all patients active in these clinics. One year later, a followup study was done. The charts of the same 1,752 patients were sought for the coding of the medications and dosages prescribed as of February, 1984. With such longitudinal techniques, it is possible to trace the actual changes over time occurring in the pharmacotherapy of patients. Coding was done on structured coding forms. For the first data collection period, coding was done by case managers who are directly involved in treatment. For the second phase, coding was done by trained coders with a ten percent coder reliability check.

The variables coded in 1983 to be used in this analysis are as follows: age; gender; ethnicity; most recent diagnosis; and prescribed medications and doses. When standard combination medications such as Triavil were prescribed, the component parts were coded separately. The 1984 coded variables include currently prescribed medications and doses, patient status (that is, active or inactive in treatment) and year treatment began in adult outpatient MHMRA clinics. Diagnosis was made by psychiatrists trained to use *DSM-III*. For the purposes of this analysis, however, diagnosis has been collapsed into eight general categories: schizophrenia, affective disorder, personality disorder, substance abuse, organic brain syndrome, other psychosis, other mental illness, and mental retardation.

Of the original 1,752 patient charts coded, 14 could not be located the second time because of obviously faulty case numbers (our only means of identification). Of the remaining 1,738 cases that could potentially be found, 1,636 (93 percent) were located. These included patients who were still under treatment (70 percent), and patients who were inactivated either at the time of the first data collection or during the subsequent year (30 percent). This particular analysis will focus upon the located patients who were active at both time periods.

Data have been analyzed using the Statistical Package for the Social Sciences. In all statistical tests, a probability of .05 is indicative of statistical significance.

RESULTS

Sample Description

The sample is composed of 1,140 patients who were active in both 1983 and 1984. Fifty-seven percent are females and 43 percent are males. The ethnic backgrounds vary: 36 percent are Anglo, 49 percent are Black, 14 percent are Hispanic, and one percent are Asian American. Ages in 1984 ranged from 18 to 91 years. The age distribution has a positive skew, with a mode of 30 years and a mean of nearly 44 years (SD = 14.2).

As we have already mentioned, these are chronic patients, most of whom have had histories in the mental health system. Years of treatment in the outpatient public facilities range from one to 17 years. The mean number of years in treatment is 6.8. The distribution is bimodal, however, with the two peaks occurring at two and nine years.

Schizophrenia is the most common primary diagnosis (60 percent), followed by affective disorder (19 percent). Personality disorder accounts for ten percent of the primary diagnoses. Substance abuse and mental retardation are infrequent diagnoses, because those patients are generally referred to other facilities. Only seven percent received secondary diagnoses. In subsequent analyses, diagnosis will refer to the primary diagnosis.

Number of Medications

As a first step in the analysis, the number of medications prescribed at each time period was compared. In both years, the number of medications ranged from zero to six. In 1983, 43 percent of the patients received two or more different medications. In 1984, the percentage increased slightly to 45 percent. Similarly, in 1983, the mean number of medications prescribed was 1.49 (SD = .77); in 1984 the mean was 1.55 (SD = .82). A Student's *t*-test detected a significant difference between the two years ($t = -2.58$; $df = 1138$; $p = .01$). This difference remains about the same (that is, .06 medications) even when patients not treated pharmacologically are excluded. Thus, it appears that there may be a slight drift towards increased polypharmacy, along with a slight increase in the amount of variation. However, one must be cautious in interpreting these results. The phenomenon of patients receiving more than one medication can be labeled as polypharmacy only if one accepts a very broad definition, such as that adopted by Odejide (1980) and Hemminki (1977). These percentages include all medications prescribed by the clinic psychiatrists. An appreciable proportion (21 percent in 1983 and 22 percent in 1984) are for ancillary medications such as anticholinergics, anticonvulsants, and other nonpsychoactive substances, including multivitamins in some instances. That is, of the patients prescribed more than one medication, only about one-half were receiving more than one psychotropic medication.

Moreover, although there was an increase in the yearly mean number of medications, one cannot conclude that all or even most of the patients experienced increased medication. Many remained the same, and some experienced a decline. To consider the patterns in number of prescriptions given, two characteristics of those patients who experienced the most change were examined: length of time in treatment and diagnosis.

The "total" column of Table 1 summarizes the extent and direction of change. The first pattern that should be noted is that for the total sample, the majority (approximately 62 percent) were stable in the number of medications given. Where change does occur, it is slightly more often an addition of one medication. This is in agreement with the results of the previous *t*-test.

Table 1. Magnitude of Change in Number of Medications by Years in Treatment

Change	Total	1 Year	2–5 Years	6–10 Years	11+ Years
≤−2	2.9	3.0	3.1	3.0	2.1
−1	13.3	18.2	12.6	13.5	13.1
0	62.3	51.5	58.2	63.6	71.7
+1	17.6	21.2	22.0	16.1	9.7
≥+2	3.9	6.1	4.1	3.8	3.4
	100 %	100%	100%	100%	100%
(*n*)	(1120)	(33)	(414)	(528)	(145)

Table 1 also contains the changes in numbers of prescriptions by the length of time in therapy. From this table it is clear that as the number of years in treatment increases, the stability in medication numbers increases considerably. Furthermore, although medication reductions stabilize after the first year, the addition of medications sharply diminishes when treatment extends over six or more years. When both variables are analyzed as continuous data (their original state), there is a low, but significant, negative correlation between the years in treatment and the difference in number of medications taken between 1983 and 1984 ($r = -.06$; $p = .04$).

Diagnosis also has an effect upon the magnitude and direction of change. Table 2 identifies the organic brain syndrome and other mental illness categories as being the most stable, while affective disorder, substance abuse, and mental retardation are the least stable. However, the pattern of change should also be noted. Schizophrenics have a roughly symmetrical pattern, while those patients with personality disorders and substance abuse have a pattern that is distinctly skewed in the direction of increase in medications. Patients with other psychoses and mental retardation have a pattern of negative skew.

These same data were submitted to an analysis of variance, in which gender and ethnicity, as well as diagnosis, were entered as independent variables, while years in treatment were entered as a covariate. In this test of an extended model, only diagnosis retains a clear effect upon the magnitude of differences. All other main effects and interaction effects are not significant. The subsequent multiple classification analysis identifies personality disorder, substance abuse, and organic brain syndrome as having a large positive difference, and other psychosis and mental retardation as having the greatest negative difference.

Changes in Medication Types

Another strategy in analysis is to identify which medication types and combinations are being prescribed more or less frequently over a one year period. Table 3 presents the frequency

Table 2. Magnitude of Change in Number of Medications by Diagnosis

Change	Total	Schizophrenia	Affective Disorder	Personality Disorder	Substance Abuse	Organic Brain Syndrome	Other Psychosis	Other Mental Illness	Mental Retardation
≤−2	2.7	3.5	1.9	0.0	4.3	2.3	7.1	4.0	0.0
−1	13.7	14.0	16.7	8.4	0.0	4.8	14.3	4.0	60.0
0	62.6	64.4	53.5	64.2	52.2	71.4	66.7	72.0	40.0
+1	17.3	14.4	23.7	24.2	39.1	16.7	7.1	16.0	0.0
≥+2	3.7	3.7	4.2	3.2	4.4	4.8	4.8	4.0	0.0
	100%	100%	100%	100%	100%	100%	100%	100%	100%
(*n*)	(1135)	(688)	(215)	(95)	(23)	(42)	(42)	(25)	(5)

Table 3. Number of Prescriptions by Year

Medication Type	1983	1984
Antipsychotics	1020	1031
Antidepressants	167	167
Antianxiety	25	31
Lithium	121	129
Sedatives	11	16
Anticholinergics	329	362
Deanol	7	0
Antiseizure	10	6
Other, nonpsychoative	13	25
Total	1703	1767

distributions of general medication types by year. As can be seen, the differences that exist between 1983 and 1984 are quite small. Moreover, the changes are evenly dispersed among medication types. In fact, there are no significant differences in the likelihood of medication types to change ($\chi^2 = 11.312$; $df = 7$; $p > .05$). It is also obvious from Table 3 that antipsychotics are by far the most often prescribed medication types, an expected result, since schizophrenia is the most frequent diagnosis in this study population. We will narrow our focus at this point to look more closely at the prescribing of these antipsychotics. Specifically, we will examine situations in which more than one antipsychotic is prescribed to a patient, and situations in which they are prescribed in combination with another psychotropic agent.

Antipsychotic Combinations

In 1984, 62 of the 952 patients (6.5 percent) treated with antipsychotics were receiving more than one of this type of medication. This is one percent more than in 1983. Most of these patients (84 percent) carry a primary diagnosis of schizophrenia. About 71 percent of the combinations involve fluphenazine decanoate (Prolixin Decanoate) plus another medication—most often either thioridazine (Mellaril) or chlorpromazine. Another 19 percent are combinations of thioridazine and some agent other than fluphenazine decanoate—most often either trifluoperazine (Stelazine) or haloperidol (Haldol).

It is noteworthy that when a medication change has occurred, the single most common change that occurred was in the addition of fluphenazine decanoate in 1984. It is interesting that this has not been accompanied by a corresponding increase in total dosage of antipsychotic medication as measured by milligrams per day in chlorpromazine equivalents, using the Davis (1974) ratios. In 1983 the average daily dose for patients taking antipsychotics was 452 mgs per day (SD = 678); in 1984 it was 473 mgs per day (SD = 690). This was not a significant increase ($t = -.82$; $df = 589$; $p = .41$).

Between Type Combinations

Of the 952 patients taking antipsychotics in 1984, 52 percent were taking only medications in this category. Another 29 percent were taking antipsychotics in combination with some non-psychotropic medication(s), usually an anticholinergic, and/or anticonvulsant agents. The percentages for the previous year were the same.

The remaining 19 percent were taking antipsychotics in combination with some other psychotropic agent. As can be seen from Figure 1, antipsychotics were used with every major category of psychotropic medication, although with radically differing frequencies. Combinations of three different other types are relatively rare. There are no instances of combinations involving four or more types. Antidepressants are the agents most frequently used in combination with antipsychotics, although there have been minor decreases in this combination over the year. Lithium, however, is also frequently found in combination with antipsychotics, and its use appears to be increasing. This is the case both in simple combinations with antipsychotics, and in combinations that include antipsychotics and antidepressants. Drug combinations do not occur evenly over the study sample. Patients taking antipsychotics alone tend most often to be diagnosed with schizo-

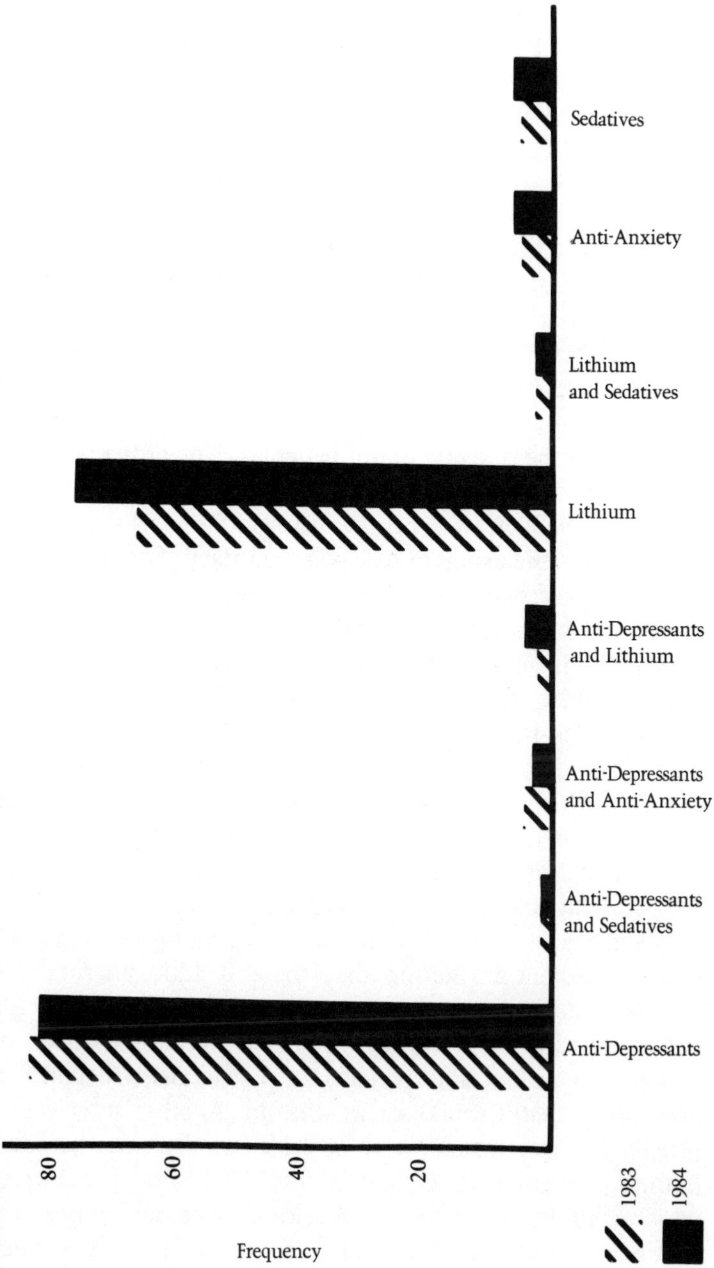

Figure 1 Medications in combination with anti-psychotics, 1983-1984.

phrenia, other psychosis, or organic brain syndrome. Patients taking the antipsychotics combined with either antidepressants or lithium tend to have diagnoses of affective disorder ($\chi^2 = 3.6884$; $df = 12$; $p > .05$).

DISCUSSION

In examining the results of our study, it is important to keep in mind the characteristics of our patient population. The majority of the patients are female, minority (mostly Black), middle aged, chronic schizophrenic, with an average of seven years in treatment. Each of these factors may be significant in analyzing our data.

Although the majority of our patients are on either no medication or on one medication, there is a sizeable proportion (43 percent in 1983) on two or more medications. This should not be interpreted as the extent of true polypharmacy, if by that term we mean the excessive combining and over-use of multiple antipsychotic and/or antidepressant medication. Table 1 includes antiparkinsonian drugs, and nonpsychotropics such as antihypertensives and anticonvulsants. We would not include combinations involving these agents as examples of polypharmacy. The rate of polypharmacy (6.5 percent) that we have detected, which involves more than one antipsychotic, is much closer to the lower rate found by Baldessarini (1984) than by Mason and associates (1977). Furthermore, the total mean dose of antipsychotics did not significantly change over the year.

When we look at antipsychotic combinations, the literature is fairly consistent in stating that there is little pharmacologic rationale for combining two or more antipsychotics (Davis 1975; Diamond et al. 1976; Hollister 1983). One exception may be a case in which a patient is responding to thioridazine (Mellaril), but needs more than the 800 mg maximum. Another antipsychotic, usually chlorpromazine, may be added to decrease the risk of retinitis pigmentosa (Prien and Coffey 1975). Another example in which combining two antipsychotics may be appropriate is the starting of a patient on treatment with fluphenazine decanoate. It may be wise to keep the patient on another antipsychotic or fluphenazine hydrochloride, as it may take 24 to 96 hours for the fluphenazine decanoate to take effect (Davis 1975). Another common instance of the combining of antipsychotics is the pairing of a piperazine phenothiazine with a more sedative aliphatic, such as chlorpromazine or the piperadine thioridazine. Hollister (1983) sees this tendency as indicative of the popular "target symptom approach," which is based on the idea that all neuroleptics are symptomatic rather than specific treatments for schizophrenia. He further states that this approach ignores the fact that all neuroleptics share a common pharmacologic action on the brain and should be equal in their therapeutic action.

Except in the case of schizoaffective illness, the use of antipsychotics with antidepressants and/or lithium may represent diagnostic uncertainty (Hollister 1975; Goodnick and Meltzer 1984). This same diagnostic confusion may also be manifested in the changes in the numbers of medications prescribed from one year to the next. It is not surprising that affective disorder, personality disorder, and substance abuse are the diagnostic categories tending toward the greatest changes. They are also categories in which diagnosis can be particularly problematic. For example, it is known that Blacks are often misdiagnosed with respect to affective disorders (Bell and Mehta 1980, 1981). Substance abuse veils the underlying disorder, again making effective psychopharmacotherapy difficult. In addition, personality disorders are difficult to diagnose, and the negative countertransference that these patients often evoke increases the tendency to medicate rather than to engage in therapy.

The correlation of number of years in treatment with greater stability in medication regimen may be interpreted as either good or bad treatment. There is a tendency in public psychiatry to maintain patients on whatever they had been taking before, with little or no effort at re-evaluation. On the other hand, this stability may reflect a continuity of care in its more favorable aspect. Stable patients may represent that group of schizophrenics known as "chronic remitting," for whom the medication regimen remains essentially the same, except during periods of exacerbation of illness (Prien and Coffey 1975). Our data do not permit a test of this.

CONCLUSION

Although, for the most part, physician prescribing patterns in the ambulatory care clinics over the year have been fairly consistent and adhered mostly to state of the art prescribing patterns, there is evidence of polypharmacy in some areas. The clinical justification for polypharmacy remains a controversial issue (Hollister 1975; Glickman 1984; Glass and Kimball 1984). Although polypharmacy could be indicated in special circumstances, it is rare that a patient needs to be maintained on antipsychotic, antidepressant, antiparkinsonian, and anxiolitic agents simultaneously. Documented instances of polypharmacy may reflect the problems of increased patient load, and limited manpower and resources inherent in public sector psychiatry. Our program has a medical school training component with third and fourth year psychiatry residents, and faculty psychiatrists as the main prescribers. This may account for our low rate of polypharmacy as compared to other rates reported in the literature. The potential of using longitudinal data on prescribing practices, and giving computer feedback to these prescribers, can have a tremendous impact on decreasing polypharmacy and other inappropriate prescribing patterns (Diamond et al. 1976; Burton 1978; Alexander et al. 1983).

In conclusion, we offer a few guidelines for long-term prescribing practices for chronic patients in the public sector. First, the physician should avoid ritualistic patterns of prescribing. Frequent assessment of the total medication picture should be made for each patient. If a previously stable patient begins to decompensate, it may be necessary to increase or to add medications temporarily until the condition improves. When there are signs of improvement, the patient should be shifted back to the maintenance level of medication.

The addition of medications ought to be accompanied by a reappraisal of all other medications, as well. It is important to keep in mind that as medications are added to the regimen, interactions may occur. The physician must be aware that other reactions may occur that could increase side effects. For example, when antiparkinsonian or antidepressant agents are added to an antipsychotic that has anticholinergic properties, the incidence of anticholinergic side effects will be additive.

The combination of several medication types may be indicative of diagnostic uncertainty. Under these circumstances, a diagnostic re-evaluation may be in order.

Persons with diagnoses of either affective disorder, personality disorder, or substance abuse (in addition to Blacks and women) may be more at risk of medication instability and/or polypharmacy. The physician should take special care in prescribing for these groups of patients.

References

Alexander B, Nasrallah HA, Perry PJ, et al: The impact of psychopharmacology education on prescribing practices. Hosp Community Psychiatry 34:1150-1154, 1983

Baldessarini RJ, Katz B, Cotton P: Dissimilar dosing with high-potency and low-potency neuroleptics. Am J Psychiatry 141:748-752, 1984

Bell C, Mehta H: Misdiagnosis of black patients with manic depressive illness. J Natl Med Assoc 72(2):141-145, 1980

Bell C, Mehta H: Misdiagnosis of black patients with manic depressive illness: second in a series. J Natl Med Assoc 73(2):101-107, 1981

Burton J: A study of the effect of computer feedback on polypharmacy. J Clin Psychiatry 39(9): 690-692, 1978

Davis JM: Dose equivalent of antipsychotic drugs. J Psychiatr Res 11:65-69, 1974

Davis JM: Overview maintenance therapy in psychiatry: schizophrenia. Am J Psychiatry 132:1237-1245, 1975

Diamond H, Tislow R, Snyder T, et al: Peer review of prescribing patterns in a CMHC. Am J Psychiatry 133:697-699, 1976

Glass RM, Kimball CP: Letter to the editor: reply to Glickman. JAMA 251:2658, 1984

Glickman L: Letter to the editor. JAMA 251:2657-2658, 1984

Goodnick PJ, Meltzer HY: Treatment of schizoaffective disorders. Schizophr Bull 10:30-48, 1984

Hemminki E: Polypharmacy among psychiatric patients. Acta Psychiatr Scand 56:347-356, 1977

Hollister L: Polypharmacy in psychiatry: is it necessary, good or bad? in Rational Psychopharmacotherapy and the Right to Treatment. Edited by Ayd FJ. Baltimore, Ayd Medical Communications Ltd, 1975

Hollister L: Clinical Pharmacology of Psychotherapeutic Drugs. 2nd edition. New York, Churchill Livingstone, 1983

Laska E, Craig TJ, Siegel C, et al: Long-term monitoring of psychopharmacological treatment in hospitalized patients, in Epidemiological Impact of Psychotropic Drugs. Edited by Tognoni G, Bellontriono C, Lader M. Amsterdam, Elsevier/North-Holland Biomedical Press, 1981

Mason AS, Nerviaro V, DeBurger RA: Patterns of antipsychotic drug use in four southeastern state hospitals. Diseases of the Nervous System 38:541-545, 1977

Odejide AO: Patterns of psychotropic drug use in a Nigerian psychiatric outpatient clinic. International Journal of Pharmacopsychiatry 15:14-23, 1980

Prien R, Coffey E: Guidelines for antipsychotic drug use. Resident and Staff Physician 9:165-172, 1975

5

The Patient Volunteer: An Alternative Approach

Ranjit C. Chacko, M.D.

5

The Patient Volunteer: An Alternative Approach

Chronic mental illness usually produces a breakdown of an individual's ability to function in the family, the work place, and often in some aspect of interpersonal relationships. Many theoretical models exist for the etiology and treatment of the most common forms of chronic mental illness; that is, schizophrenia and the major affective disorders. For the most part, they include genetic, biochemical, psychological, behavioral, familial, and sociocultural models. During the past 50 years we have seen the focus shift among these theoretical models, with specific treatment interventions designed to address them. Yet most experienced clinicians who treat chronic patients recognize that the needs of this group of patients are multiple, complex, and often overlapping. Besides traditional outpatient activities such as diagnostic assessment, medication maintenance, and psychotherapy, these patients also require active case management, socialization experiences, vocational rehabilitation or employment, low cost housing, and financial support at one time or another. In most instances, community mental health services have not been able to respond to these overwhelming needs that were created by the deinstitutionalization movement.

Freud (1939) wrote that work has a greater effect than any other technique of living in the direction of binding the individual more closely to reality; in one's work, at least, one is securely attached to a part of reality, the human community. Only 25 years ago, two out of every three hours of labor in mental hospitals were performed by unpaid patients. These chronic mental patients operated food services, housekeeping, laundry services, worked on paint crews, and maintained the grounds of state hospitals with minimal supervision for many years (Brooks 1981). Yet, with the advent of deinstitutionalization, these valuable experiences and therapeutic gains were disregarded by clinicians for many years before they were rediscovered in the community support program (CSP) models and the lodge programs of the 1970s (Beard et al. 1982). Many studies have clearly demonstrated the superiority of work experiences in the degree of autonomy and independence achieved by chronic patients (Christensen 1974; Lamb and Goertzel 1972).

A clinical program will be described in this chapter that has attempted to address the needs of the chronic patient by making creative and innovative program changes within a fairly traditional ambulatory community mental health setting. The Mid-City Clinic is one of five ambulatory community based public sector clinics in Houston that is affiliated with the Baylor College of Medicine, Community and Social Psychiatry Programs. The clinic serves a population of state hospital and general hospital-discharged chronic patients—with an active case load of 650 patients—and offers a wide range of clinical services on site. They include diagnostic assessment, medication maintenance, individual, family, and group psychotherapy, case management, and day treatment activities.

The volunteer program at the Mid-City Clinic was initiated in early 1983, following about six months of planning and discussion by the staff. Initial resistance to the development of such a program was fairly strong. The staff expressed two major concerns: Patients functioning as volunteers in the clinic would cause blurring of staff-patient roles and destroy well-established therapeutic alliances. The clinical staff also felt that they were too busy with direct patient care activities and suggested that it was more appropriate for the recently established CSP to assist the clinic with these activities.

Agreement was finally reached to try the project as a one year pilot program. Many staff members shared their experiences of patients showing steady progress in a structured day treatment program, only to regress weeks later because of failure to survive in a competitive work place (due to loss of work, or to repeated rejection by potential employers). Patients often withdrew, became less involved in clinical activities, and showed symptomatic relapses. At the same time, the local CSP became flooded with new referrals within six months of its inception, and developed a waiting list for new intakes. Clinical staff became more receptive to the idea when the use of volunteers in clerical support roles was discussed, especially when it was suggested that they could help with paper work and filing in the clinic. Support staff welcomed such help in the patient waiting area as directing patients to various activities, and in the never-ending task of making coffee for patients.

The program was sponsored by four staff members (a psychologist, a social worker, the clerical supervisor, and a nurse) under the overall direction of the clinical director (a psychiatrist). The staff sponsors were responsible for selecting suitable patients, formulating goals for the programs, and promoting group cohesiveness by facilitating communication. The first group consisted of 14 patients: seven bipolars and seven chronic schizophrenics; there were eight females and six males; all of the patients had long past psychiatric histories, with at least three hospitalizations and poor work adjustments.

The initial goals of the volunteer program were: *1.* to provide opportunities in the clinic for patients to participate in a variety of work related activities as volunteers; *2.* to reduce the 'sick dependent role' that chronic patients generally assume in traditional clinical settings; *3.* to increase the self-esteem and autonomous functioning of patients by providing opportunities for successful work experiences; *4.* to improve the work adjustment, social skills, and money management of these patients; and *5.* to provide 'normal role models' to the more severely regressed patients in the clinic.

All patients enrolled in the program were oriented to the role of volunteer by staff from the local Red Cross. A brief lecture and film covered such areas as the meaning and responsibility of volunteerism, ethics, confidentiality, commitment, and employment credit. Patients were then given a general job description and identification badges by the Red Cross.

The volunteer program at the Mid-City Clinic has sponsored four separate ongoing activities at the clinic:

1. The Breakfast Program
2. A Patient Education Program
3. The Clerical Program
4. The Geriatric Patient Assistance Program

THE BREAKFAST PROGRAM

The Breakfast Program was begun in early 1983, and has provided a hot breakfast in the clinic kitchen for a reasonable cost to patients, staff, and, in the past six months, to other occupants of the office building (including personnel from various private companies and offices of the state and city). The patient volunteers have been responsible for grocery shopping, menu planning, food preparation, kitchen maintenance, cashiering, accounting, and advertising activities for this program. Assistance and direction in such matters as budgeting, food preparation, and services necessary to meet health standards have been provided by a staff member from food services at the local psychiatric hospital. The program has been extremely successful in many respects. The volunteers, with minimal assistance, have varied the breakfast menu and advertised the program effectively. A patient volunteer who was an unemployed artist was responsible for designing attractive posters that were used on all floors of the building. The group enlisted the help of a staff sponsor to establish a bank account, and has regularly deposited profits from the sale of breakfasts. Volunteers have used these funds appropriately to replace worn out kitchen appliances, and to organize recreational group activities for themselves; that is, movies, trips, and so forth. An important by-product of this program has been the education of other occupants of our office building about chronic mental patients, and their ability to function in normal work roles. More recently, a conference of CSPs asked this group to provide meals to fifty participants for four luncheon meetings. The volunteers were excited about this opportunity to prove themselves outside the clinic setting.

THE PATIENT EDUCATION PROGRAM

The Patient Education Program conducts classes on three half-days a week. These classes are available to patients at the clinic who want to further their education. Lack of education is a common problem in chronic mental patients: their serious psychopathology is what usually causes them to fail within the school system. A teacher from the local community college has provided ongoing consultation and has obtained donations of educational materials to assist volunteers in establishing this program. Two patient volunteers, both retired school teachers, have provided tutoring to 15 patients in the clinic for the past nine months. Four patients have been successful at completing their General Equivalency Diploma (GED) through this program in the past six months. Many others have used this opportunity to brush up on language and math skills in order to feel more competent in the workplace.

THE CLERICAL PROGRAM

Patient volunteers are involved in a variety of clerical support activities under the direction of the clinic clerical supervisor. Volunteers serve as receptionists at the front desk, organize new patient folders with forms, complete direct service logs, help with duplicating material, and assist in directing patients to various activities in the clinic.

THE GERIATRIC PATIENT ASSISTANCE PROGRAM

Two volunteers, both patients who were previously employed in health related fields, have provided assistance to clinical staff and patients at the geriatric clinic. These volunteers have recorded patients' blood pressures and weights for routine monitoring purposes. They have also helped geriatric patients, who are less mobile, to fill their prescriptions by going to the local pharmacy during clinic hours. More recently, a volunteer, with the aid of the clinic nurse, has organized a "stay young through fitness" exercise program for geriatric patients.

OUTCOME

Twenty-four patient volunteers have been involved in the program since it was started 18 months ago. Seventeen patients are currently active, and five patients have gone on to full-time work. One patient returned to a community college to further his education, and another older patient has become a full-time volunteer in a local hospital. Two patients experienced exacerbations of their psychotic symptoms during this period and required hospitalization. They have since returned to the volunteer program and have resumed their activities. The volunteer group meets weekly at lunchtime to review the week's activities with staff sponsors, to discuss potential problems, and to plan future events. The group has recently instituted a four week probationary period for new volunteers, where attendance at the weekly planning meeting and involvement in the breakfast program is mandatory. The patients have also become much less dependent on staff members for direction, and have utilized supervision appropriately in most instances.

The expected problem of role confusion in volunteers became apparent early in the development of the program. Volunteers were frequently confused about their dual roles as patients and as volunteers in the clinic. The patients initially saw themselves as an elite patient group and, later, as assistants to various staff members. Sometimes, volunteers became inappropriately overinvolved with acutely ill patients at the clinic and interfered with the work of clinical staff. On a few occasions, volunteers requested attendance at staff meetings and at inservice training programs, because the posted agenda sounded interesting to them.

FUTURE DIRECTIONS

Plans for expansion of this program model are now underway. The group plans to develop new activities and to involve larger numbers of patients. One of their ideas is to develop a clothing resale shop, in which clothes that are donated to the clinic are repaired and sold to patients at low cost. Another plan is to utilize the special skills of certain volunteer group members in music, painting, and language, in the development of a leisure learning program for other patients at the clinic.

References

Beard JH, Propst RN, Malamud TJ: The Fountain House model of psychosocial rehabilitation. Psychosocial Rehabilitation Journal 5(1)47-53, Jan. 1982

Brooks GW: Vocational rehabilitation, in The Chronic Mentally Ill. New York, Human Sciences Press, 1981

Christensen JK: A five year follow up of male schizophrenics: evaluation of factors influencing success and failure in the community. Acta Psychiatr Scand 50:60-72, 1974

Freud S: Civilization and Its Discontents. Hogarth Press, London, 1939

Lamb HR, Goertzel V: High expectations of long term ex-state patients. Am J Psychiatry 129(4):471-475, 1972

6

Legal Issues in the Care of the Chronic Patient

Seth W. Silverman, M.D.
Aaron H. Fink, M.D.

6

Legal Issues in the Care of the Chronic Patient

In the latter half of the 19th century, Freud's heretical views began to have an impact on law and religion. Coinciding with this incipient psychological revolution was the reclassification of many 'deviant' behaviors (such as substance abuse and sex crimes) that were formerly treated by the courts as psychiatric maladies. Recently the pendulum has swung the other way, with the law having an impact on psychiatry, with particular emphasis on the chronic mental patient. Many patients are, once again, being 'treated' by the legal system.

This influence has not always been welcomed by psychiatrists. The law seeks to arrive at justice through an adversarial contest. By design, there is a winner and a loser. This is divergent from the field of psychiatry, in which there is an attempt to promote health (justice) for all patients (contestants). In addition, it is alien to the medical profession to have external forces intrude so regularly and with such authority into the care of patients. Some individuals have accused the judicial system of practicing medicine with the wrong graduate degree.

It is the goal of this chapter to examine the ways in which legal decisions have affected the care of chronic psychiatric patients. The issues to be examined will be those of commitment, right to treatment, least restrictive alternative, confidentiality, malpractice, competency, and the right to refuse treatment.

COMMITMENT

The state's power to commit individuals has two theoretical bases: *parens patriae* ("father of his country"), and the police powers doctrine (Slovenko 1980). The doctrine of *parens patriae* holds that a person who is mentally ill and in need of treatment may be committed for that person's own benefit. The police powers doctrine is invoked for individuals who are mentally ill and are felt to be dangerous to others.

All current state statutes require mental illness as a threshold criterion for civil commitment. There is, however, no single legal definition of mental illness (Stromberg 1982). In some states, statutes enumerate a series of psychiatric conditions; other states have very loose definitions. Recently, the courts have begun to show a willingness to look beyond diagnostic labels and to examine the facts on which the diagnosis was based. For example, in *re D.W.H.* (1980), the court heard testimony that a dissociative reaction is a mental illness "only when it creates symptoms or dysfunction, or when it is maladaptive." The Court reviewed the patient's recent behavior and did not hold "that the dissociative reaction is a psychiatric disorder in D.W.H.'s case." The patient was subsequently discharged.

Most courts and state laws have come to require dangerousness to others or to oneself as a standard for commitment. This trend has occurred as a misinterpretation of the *O'Connor v. Donaldson* (1975) decision. Kenneth Donaldson was committed at his parent's request when he was 49 years old. He had been complaining that there was a conspiracy to poison him. Whenever the hospital planned to discharge him, his fearful elderly parents objected. His 19 writs of habeas corpus (a legal petition used to gain freedom of a person in custody) were denied by the court. Following the death of his parents the hospital did not discharge him, because the hospital administration thought it was inappropriate to place him in the custody of a nonrelative. The Supreme Court subsequently ruled that a "finding of 'mental illness' alone cannot justify a state's locking up a person against his will and keeping him indefinitely in simple custodial confinement" (p. 575). The patient was then discharged.

In cases where dangerousness has been used as a justification for commitment, the question as to whether a "recent overt act, attempt, or threat" is needed for commitment (Stromberg 1982) has been repeatedly raised. In *Lessard v. Schmidt* (1972, 1974, 1976) the court held that a recent act was required, but the question of how recent was left unanswered.

A related, unsettled question is whether commitment can be justified when there is no overt threat or act, but when the person has a mental illness (for example, psychotic depression) that has a high correlation with violence (Stromberg 1982).

How near in the future the predicted harm is likely to occur is another unresolved dilemma. Various state statutes specify "imminent" or "real and present" or "in the near future," without specific criteria.

The landmark case that first examined the procedural issues specific to involuntary civil commitment was *Lessard v. Schmidt* (1972). Although it was never affirmed by the U.S. Supreme Court, *Lessard* has served as a model for subsequent litigation. Citing the "massive curtailment of liberty" associated with commitment, the court developed a series of procedural requirements; these included a preliminary hearing before a judge within 48 hours of detention, a full hearing within 14 days, representation by a legal advocate throughout the process, and the option of a jury trial at the full hearing. Other courts have followed these recommendations.

In *French v. Blackburn* (1977), a federal district court gave psychiatrists significant decision-making abilities when it let stand a North Carolina statute that allowed an individual to be held for up to ten days without a full hearing, after being certified by two physicians. The court reasoned that involuntary commitment was a "hybrid proceeding, which although it involves a deprivation of liberty, the very purpose of that deprivation is not solely to protect society but also has a purpose: the protection, treatment and aid of an individual who cannot or will not protect himself." On appeal, the Supreme Court (1979) affirmed the finding without a full hearing or a written decision.

More courts and, consequently, more state legislatures, have chosen to follow the reasoning and conclusion of *Lessard* as opposed to those of *French*. The Supreme Court has not taken a clear stand, yet their affirmation without written opinion of

French suggests that commitment proceedings need not be run like criminal proceedings for constitutional due process requirements to be met.

An important issue in judicial matters is the standard of proof required. For conviction in civil trials, a "preponderance of evidence" standard is employed, which is generally understood to mean a degree of certainty of at least 51 percent. The "beyond a reasonable doubt" standard used in criminal cases is generally believed to mean a 95-99 percent degree of certainty. In *Addington v. Texas* (1979), the Supreme Court found that individuals could be committed for indefinite periods only on the basis of at least "clear and convincing" evidence. This standard is intermediate between the "preponderance of evidence" standard and the "beyond a reasonable doubt" standard, and is generally accepted to mean a 75 percent degree of certainty.

While the jury or court uses the standard of "clear and convincing" evidence, the psychiatrist is often asked to predict the likelihood that the person will engage in dangerous behavior. Although the degree of likelihood that is required is often undefined, it may vary from "substantial risk" to "substantial probability." Thus, as Stromberg (1982) points out, commitments for dangerousness are probably based on a complicated two step probability equation: "the seriousness of the potential harm," as well as the likelihood of the occurrence.

The interaction of the legal system with the mental health system in the area of commitment has resulted in many shifts. Statutory definitions of mental illness have become more conceptually sophisticated and precise. The courts have moved beyond diagnostic labels to examine underlying data. The courts expect more evidence of specific threats and acts. This trend, however, may be short-lived; the Supreme Court in *Project Release v. Prevost* (1982) ruled that an overt act was not required.

RIGHT TO TREATMENT

Under the United States Constitution, the protection of liberty is guaranteed with no specific reference to rights to services. The courts have recently interpreted the Constitution as providing for a 'right to treatment' for certain psychiatric patients.

In 1966, *Rouse v. Cameron* became the first judicial decision to recognize a right to treatment. Rouse was a criminal defendant found innocent by reason of insanity, but who was subsequently committed and held for a period considerably longer than he would have served if found guilty of the crime. In his habeas corpus proceeding, Judge Bazelon invoked a newly enacted civil commitment statute that conferred a right to treatment. In dicta (nonbinding judicial opinion) he went on to assert that all involuntarily committed patients might have this same right based on the constitutional provisions of due process, equal protection, and freedom from cruel and unusual punishment.

Nason v. Superintendent of Bridgewater State Hospital (1968) was the first court case to recognize a constitutional right to treatment. The case, involving a criminally committed patient, held that the constitutional guarantees of due process and equal protection required clinically appropriate treatment. The court failed to delineate how it came to such a conclusion.

In *Wyatt v. Stickney* (Walls 1982), the principle of a right to treatment for the civilly committed was first articulated. *Wyatt* began as a class action suit filed against Alabama officials. The goal of the suit was to improve conditions at two state hospitals and a state school. In his first of four opinions, Judge Johnson argued, "To deprive any citizen of his or her liberty upon the altruistic theory that the confinement is for humane, therapeutic reasons and then fail to provide adequate treatment violates the very fundamental of due process." Not only did Judge Johnson provide a clearly articulated, constitutionally based right to treatment doctrine, but also a comprehensive set of minimum clinical standards. The standards included "1. a humane psychological and physical environment; 2. qualified staff in numbers sufficient to administer adequate treatment; and 3. individualized treatment plans."

O'Connor v. Donaldson (1975) was the first right-to-treatment case to reach the Supreme Court. The court chose to sidestep the right to treatment issue, and instead ruled that civil liability could arise when the state held without treatment a nondangerous individual who had others in the community willing to provide for his needs. This ruling served to deflate the importance of the lower court's finding of a constitutional right to treatment.

While the rulings in the right-to-treatment cases have been influential, Mills (1982) points out, "The action of the cases has not been in their holdings, but in their remedies. Most right-to-treatment cases have been settled by consent decree, without formal adjudications" (p. 365). The consent decree is a formal contract between two parties, which is implemented and enforced by the court. The process of arriving at a consent decree avoids a judicial ruling on either the facts of the case or any constitutional legal questions (that is, the right to treatment).

There are several problems with the use of consent decrees (Stone 1977), the most important being that consent decrees often prove to be too specific and inflexible to obtain the desired changes. Despite these and other limitations, there have been over 30 consent decrees issued since 1972 (Mills 1982). Their importance has been greatly exaggerated; and patient care, especially in public institutions, has been unaffected.

LEAST RESTRICTIVE ALTERNATIVE

The *Wyatt v. Stickney* decision and others like it led to court-ordered changes in state mental hospitals. According to some activist lawyers, these changes were not sufficient to rectify the problems in the mental health system. As a result, the Mental Health Law Project (a public interest law firm) began to press for a shift toward community as opposed to state hospital care in the mid-1970s. They developed and promoted the doctrine of the least restrictive alternative to further their goals (Klein 1982).

In the *Lake v. Cameron* (1966) case, Judge Bazelon wrote that the trial judge should have explored other alternatives before committing an elderly woman to St. Elizabeths Hospital for custodial care. He did not find a right to any alternative form of care. Chief Justice Burger, who at that time was sitting on the Court of Appeals, wrote a strong dissent, arguing that the issue of alternative placements was a clinical and not a judicial decision.

Recognizing that the mentally retarded generated more public sympathy and support than the mentally ill, the initial class two action suits were aimed at grossly inadequate state schools. Rather than fight the suits, most states agreed to the formulation of consent decrees.

After years of legal planning and maneuvering, the stage was set for *Halderman v. Pennhurst State School and Hospital* (1977). Following four years of legal arguments, the trial court held that the constitution gave the right to a least restrictive alternative, and ordered the closing of Pennhurst and the community placement of over 1,000 mentally retarded individuals. The judge, by citing case after case precedent, made it appear that there was a generally recognized constitutional right to a least restrictive alternative.

The decision was appealed to the Supreme Court, which remanded the case for further consideration.

In *Romeo v. Youngblood* (1980), the Court of Appeals for the Third Circuit upheld the doctrine of least restrictive alternative when applied to the treatment setting. The Supreme Court has agreed to hear the case.

When evaluating the impact of these cases, it is important to realize that only legislatures can back up patient rights by allocating the necessary funds (Klein 1982). Six years after the decision involving St. Elizabeths Hospital, only a handful of patients have been placed in the community. Yet the doctrine of least restrictive alternative is recognized by the majority of states.

CONFIDENTIALITY

Confidentiality is the legal and ethical obligation on the part of the physician to protect and safeguard information obtained in the course of treatment. Laws on confidentiality not only limit the ability of the physician to divulge information about a given patient without his or her knowledge, but actually limit the court's ability to intrude upon the therapeutic relationship (Weiner and Shuman 1983).

Hippocrates is the first physician recorded to recognize the importance of confidentiality in the therapeutic relationship. "Whatsoever things I see or hear concerning the life of men in my attendances on the sick, or even part therefrom which ought not to be noised abroad, I will silence thereon, consenting such things to be as holy secrets." Hippocrates did not talk about an absolute confidence but a relative confidence when he states that "which ought not to be noised abroad." He leaves it up to the discretion of the physician to decide when information obtained during the course of a patient-physician interaction can be divulged. The question of how confidential information really is has become a complex and difficult problem for psychiatrists in recent years. Physicians have been successfully sued for either divulging too little or too much information.

The privileged and protected status of the patient-physician relationship is one of many special relationships protected by law in our society. The law also provides protection in other instances, including the following: *1.* individuals cannot be forced to incriminate themselves; *2.* spouses cannot be forced to testify against each other; *3.* the lawyer-client relationship cannot be violated, except in the most unusual and extreme circumstances. Society has deemed certain information confidential in some relationships that it would otherwise feel compelled to examine. However, this privilege has always been relative and can be rescinded under certain circumstances. Indeed, the medical profession has enjoined this right, by making mandatory the reporting of various infectious diseases such as smallpox, venereal disease, acts of violence (specifically gunshot wounds), as well as child and adult abuse.

The limits of the confidence of the patient-physician relationship and, more specifically, the patient-therapist relationship, has come under closer scrutiny in recent years by the courts, with the major impact of these decisions being to clarify the limits of therapeutic confidentiality. Most of these decisions have emanated from the private sector.

In the case of *Doe v. Roe* (1977), a psychiatrist was successfully sued because his book about the treatment of one of his patients was found to violate the right to privacy; the book was written in such a manner that the patient could be identified.

The most widely publicized case in recent times regarding the issue of confidentiality is that of the *Tarasoff* ruling (*Tarasoff v. University of California, 1976)*. Although most therapists are aware that this ruling exists, studies have shown that the findings of the court are commonly misunderstood (Runck 1984). The *Tarasoff* ruling emanated from the death of Tatania Tarasoff, who was killed by Prosenjit Poddar while she was a student at the University of California. The suit was brought by the family of Ms. Tarasoff, who alleged that Poddar had seen a psychologist at the university clinic, who became concerned about Poddar's potential for violence. The psychologist asked the campus police to involuntarily commit Poddar.

Poddar was briefly detained by campus police but was released because they felt he posed no danger. The entire matter was subsequently dropped by the psychologist at the request of his superiors. Six months later, Poddar killed Tarasoff. The California Supreme Court eventually ruled that if the facts of the case were proven true, and some action by the staff could have prevented the murder, then the university could theoretically be held liable and accountable. The 1976 ruling stated that warning potential victims was one of many possible means available to the therapist to alleviate the problem.

A recent study found that most therapists are aware of the decision, but are ill-informed of its meaning. The majority believe that the ruling required a warning rather than "reasonable care" guideline, and thought they were legally bound by the ruling. In addition, the proportion of therapists who believed the ruling obligated them to warn whenever a threat was made, regardless of the perceived danger, was one-fourth (Runck 1984). Subsequent court decisions have disagreed as to how clear a danger must be before a therapist is obligated to take action.

The John Hinckley, Jr. case is probably the most widely publicized case regarding mental illness and confidentiality in recent times (*Brady v. Hopper,* 1983). Mr. Hinckley attempted to assassinate President Reagan in the spring of 1981. He failed, but succeeded in wounding President Reagan's press secretary, James Brady. Mr. Brady was shot in the head and suffered brain damage.

He brought suit against Dr. Hopper, who had been treating Hinckley. Brady alleged that the physician should have been able to predict and/or prevent Mr. Hinckley's actions. According to the case, Hinckley's parents brought him to see Dr. Hopper in 1980 after a reported suicide attempt. Dr. Hopper treated Hinckley with diazepam and biofeedback. The plaintiffs charged that the treatment Dr. Hopper prescribed was inadequate, and may have even exacerbated Hinckley's condition. They also stated that had Dr. Hopper been more thorough and extensive in his evaluation, he would have found out that Hinckley was obsessed with the movie "Taxi Driver," had a library on political assassinations, and a fascination with guns and with the actress Jodie Foster.

The court ruled that even if the facts of the case were true, there was insufficient evidence to conclude that Hinckley was a grave risk to himself or to others of sufficient degree to require Dr. Hopper to take action. In the words of the court, "human behavior is simply too unpredictable, and the field of psychotherapy presently too inexact, to so greatly expand this scope of the therapist's need only to respond to protect specific individuals from specific threats."

The Supreme Court of the State of Washington recently rejected the "specific threats to specific victims" doctrine necessitating action, stating that a psychiatrist has the duty to protect any individual who might be endangered by his or her patient (*Peterson v. Washington,* 1983). The case involved an individual who struck the defendant after running a red light at approximately 60 mph, reportedly under the influence of a variety of intoxicants. In addition, he was on probation for second degree burglary, the terms of which included that he remain drug-free and participate in therapy. Five days prior to the accident, the defendant had been released from the state hospital where he had been receiving psychiatric care for having emasculated himself. On admission, he was diagnosed as having a "schizophrenic reaction paranoid type with depressive features," secondary to angel dust. He was put on a major tranquilizer and committed for a period of up to 14 days. At the end of commitment he was discharged, at which time his diagnosis was changed from schizophrenia to a schizophrenic-like reaction due to angel dust. Five days later the accident occurred. The court stated that because he was a potentially dangerous individual with unpredictable behavior, the psychiatrist should have taken greater responsibility to protect any potentially involved individuals.

The rulings from the preceding cases appear to be contradictory, as the specific threat–specific victim doctrine dominates in some courts, and the nonspecific threat–nonspecific victim doctrine rules in other instances.

Chronic patients may find confidences violated even when there is no perceived threat of danger. Increased utilization and accessibility of records due to fiscal accountability, computerization, administrative and clinical peer review, research protocols, and greater paraprofessional involvement may make it inevitable that psychiatric records have a widespread readership. This pertains especially to those patients who receive their care in an institutional setting (clinic, public sector, halfway house, or hospital). These individuals may find the nuances of their therapeutic relationship increasingly accessible to individuals other than their therapists (Harvard 1984). The implications, both clinical and legal, have yet to be ascertained.

The right to privacy and confidentiality has come under increasing scrutiny by the law. The resultant decisions have laid out more specific and, at times, conflicting guidelines as to when divulgences function as a necessity or as a bane.

COMPETENCE

In the 17th century, those individuals who were thought to be poor, blind, heretics, pagans, female relatives of criminals, the deaf and dumb, slaves, people with poor reputations, males under 14, and females under 12, were automatically judged to be incompetent to give testimony in court. This was a precursor of our current legal system with regard to the legal concept of competence (Walker 1968).

Competence is a legal term by which courts decide whether an individual understands the situation he is in and can make a logical, rational, and coherent decision. In our society, once individuals reach a certain minimum age (the age varies with the perceived complexity and maturation required to perform a task), they are assumed to be competent. Competence is a selective ability to perform certain specific functions. Areas of competency include the ability to make out a will, sign a contract, stand trial, handle finances, get married or divorced, perform as a witness, resist the treatment recommendations of a psychiatrist, and participate in court (Smith 1983).

English common law is probably responsible for our current system of determining competence. When defendants refused to enter pleas in their behalf, English judges needed a way to determine whether an individual was 'mute of malice' or was mentally ill. The peine forte et dur was the court's solution, which consisted of the accused individual slowly being pressed to death under increasing weight until he decided to enter a plea on his own behalf. This unusually compelling process was not officially abolished until 1772.

During the 18th and 19th centuries, the press was replaced by a more humane process. The defendant was required to understand the charges against him, and was required to effectively participate in his own defense (Walker 1968).

Current competency laws are the result of the influence of Issac Grey, who stated that the trial or sentence of an individual charged with a crime in which the plea of insanity has been entered be delayed, so that a physician could observe the accused (Smith 1983).

There are three cases that are particularly pertinent to this issue (Smith 1983). Milton Dusky was a 33-year-old male who was charged with kidnapping and attempted rape of a 15-year-old high school student. Dusky had a chronic psychiatric illness diagnosed as "schizophrenic reactions, chronic undifferentiated type." At his hearing, a psychiatrist testified that although Dusky had a chronic history and guarded prognosis, he was not grossly impaired if he continued to take his chlorpromazine. In addition, a government psychiatrist who had treated Dusky prior to the incident testified during the trial that Dusky understood the charges against him but could not participate in his defense in a constructive manner. The judge subsequently ruled that the patient was competent, and Dusky was convicted in 1959 and sentenced to a 45-year jail term. His case was appealed on the grounds that his competency, as well as other issues related to his insanity defense, were not properly addressed. The Supreme Court found the defendant competent and established the following criteria for competency: an individual must have "sufficient present ability to consult with his lawyer with a reasonable degree of understanding, and have a rational as well as a factual understanding of the proceedings against him" (*Dusky v. U.S.* 1961).

The case was tried again in 1960 and the lawyer agreed that his client was then in much better condition. The plea of not guilty by reason of insanity was re-entered, but the patient was found guilty and sentenced to only 20 years.

The question of whether an individual is either competent or incompetent can be raised by the prosecutor, the defense attorney, or the judge. Because ramifications of such an evaluation can be harsh (such as precluding the possibility of bail and increasing the pretrial time), a competency evaluation can be perceived as punitive. As a result, the issue is often not raised when it might be. In addition, competency evaluations may be stigmatizing, and individuals may prefer to be tagged as criminals rather than to be labeled as mental patients. Even if a court does ask for an evaluation and finds the individual incompetent, the sentencing (prescription) is for the individual to receive treatment (usually in a state institution) until competency returns. The possibility of a greater or undefined stay in a mental hospital, as opposed to a fixed time period in jail, may make the life of a convict appear more appealing than that of a mental patient. This was contrary to Jack Nicholson's original understanding in the movie "One Flew Over the Cuckoo's Nest."

In the case of *Pate v. Robinson,* Mr. Robinson was convicted of brutally murdering his wife, Flossy Mae Ward. Robinson's defense attorney postulated that his sanity was suspect in light of his long history of violent behavior, including one child killing and other antisocial behavior (*Pate v. Robinson* 1966).

During the course of the trial, an expert witness testified that

Robinson understood the charge against him and was able to participate in the trial in a manner that was to his own benefit. A formal competency evaluation was not requested. The defense lawyer, however, asked for a continuance for further psychiatric evaluation that was denied, with the judge stating that Robinson was "mentally alert." He was found to have a constitutional right for a competency hearing; the judge's courtroom evaluation was insufficient.

The question of whether individuals who are found incompetent can be held indefinitely or until they return to competency was tested by the case of *Jackson v. Indiana* (1972).

A 27-year-old deaf mute named Theon Jackson was charged with stealing $9.00 (Smith 1983). After a plea of not guilty was entered on his behalf, a competency evaluation was ordered. The psychiatrists concluded that Mr. Jackson could neither understand the nature of the charges brought against him nor assist in his own defense. They also reported that these abilities would probably never be acquired by Mr. Jackson. He was found incompetent and ordered hospitalized until he became competent, at which time he was to stand trial. His lawyer appealed, stating that the findings of incompetency had the effect of institutionalizing his patient for life without due process.

In 1977 the Supreme Court held that "Indiana cannot constitutionally commit the petitioner for an indefinite period simply on account of his incompetency," and ordered the state to release Jackson or institute civil commitment proceedings.

The preceding three cases of *Dusky v. U.S.*, *Pate v. Robinson*, and *Jackson v. Indiana* clearly establish the right to a competency determination, the criteria for such an evaluation, as well as the limits of such an evaluation. Individuals with a chronic psychiatric illness are also theoretically assured 'due process' before being tried for a crime.

Refusal of Psychiatric Treatment

The ability of a committed patient to refuse treatment was tested in the cases of *Rennie v. Klein* (1983) and *Rogers v. Okin* (1979) (previously *Mills v. Rogers*). The patient refused treatment (medications) on a "right to privacy." In the Rennie case, the federal district judge ruled that patients could refuse antipsychotics as long as the patient was not a danger to himself or to others. The court stated that patients have a right to be free from and to obtain judicial relief for unjustified intrusion on personal security. The court also found major tranquilizers to pose "significant risks to the patient." Another particularly controversial element of the decision was the court's statement that requires treatment to occur in the "least restrictive alternative."

The *Rogers v. Okin* (1979) district court ruling was similar. The Supreme Court has refused to hear either of these cases. The ways in which treatment of the chronic mentally ill will be affected has yet to be determined.

CONCLUSION

With increasing regularity, the legal system has continued to intrude into the psychiatrist-patient relationship. The effects on the care of the chronic patient have been largely theoretical, and the progeny of the current forced legal-psychiatric union are still restive.

With regard to commitment proceedings, an individual must either present a danger to himself or to others in order to require involuntary hospitalization. This was established in the *parens patriae* and police powers doctrine. The degree of danger that an individual presents, as well as how that fact is determined, is as yet unclear. The right to a competency determination, the criteria and limitations of such an evaluation before a trial, have been clearly established. Chronic mental patients frequently lack the resources to assure their own due process, and the courts have attempted to solve this problem.

The courts have also determined that there is a right to treatment, a right to refuse treatment, and a right to treatment in the least restrictive manner. The specific methods of implementation of such global edicts have not been clearly elucidated.

In summary, the judicial system has become more involved in the care of chronic mental patients. There has been an attempt to supplant clinical decisions with judicial decree. Implementation was largely theoretical, as relatively little expertise and resources accompanied the much-heralded proclamations. Currently the legal system appears to be less interested than it has been in the chronic mentally ill, and the pendulum seems to be in motion again. Perhaps psychiatrists of the 1980s will be able to demonstrate leadership and expertise in the care of the chronic mentally ill, roles that the legal system so unsuccessfully attempted to usurp in the previous two decades.

References

Addington v. Texas, 441 U.S. 418 (1979)

Brady v. Hopper 52 USLW 2215 USDC Colo (9/14/83)

Brooks AD: The legal considerations of medication refusals. Legal Aspects of Psychiatric Practice 1(1):1–8, August 1984

Doe v. Roe, 400 NYS 2d 668 (1977)

Dusky v. U.S., 295 F 2d 743 (8 Circ, 1961)

Freishtat Harvey W: View from the nation's courts. J Clin Psychopharmacol 4 (2) 111-112, 1984

French v. Blackburn, 428 F. Supp. 1351 (M.D., N.C., 1977)

Grob GN: Mental Institutions in America: Social Policy to 1857. New York, Free Press, 1973

Halderman v. Pennhurst State School and Hospital, 446 F. Supp. 1295 (E.D. Pa., 1977)

Harvard J: Protecting Confidentiality. Br Med J 288: April 14, 1984

In re D.W.H., 411 N.W. 2d 721 (Ind. Ct. App. 1980)

Jackson v. *Indiana,* 406 U.S. 715; 92 S.C., 1845 (1972)

Klein J: The least restrictive alternative: more about less, in Psychiatry Update: The American Psychiatric Association Annual Review, Volume One. Edited by Grinspoon L. Washington, D. C., American Psychiatric Press, 1982

Lake v. *Cameron,* 364 F. 2d 657 (1966)

Lentz S: Mental health lawyers (a letter to the editor). Hosp Community Psychiatry 34:853, 1983

Lessard v. *Schmidt*, 349 F. Supp. 1078 (E.D. Wis. 1972)

Lessard v. *Schmidt*, 414 U.S. 472 (1974)

Lessard v. *Schmidt*, 413 F. Supp. 1318 (E.D. Wis. 1976)

Logan v. *Araffeh,* 346 F. Supp. 1265 (D. Conn, 1972)

Mills M: The right to treatment: little law but much impact, in Psychiatry Update: The American Psychiatric Association Annual Review, Volume One. Edited by Grinspoon L. Washington, D.C., American Psychiatric Press, 1982

Nason v. *Superintendent of Bridgewater State Hospital*, 353 Mass. 604, 233 N.E. 2d 908 (1968)

O'Connor v. *Donaldson*, 422 U.S. 563, 575 (1975)

Pate v. *Robinson,* 383 U.S. 375; 86 S. LT 836 (1966)

Perr Irwin N: Famous and Notorious Cases, Publications and Privacy. Bull Am Acad Psychiatry Law 11 (3):207-213, 1983

Peterson v. *State of Washington,* 52, USLW 2258 (11/8/83)

Project Release v. *Prevost*, 551 F. Supp. 1298 (E.D. N.Y. 1982)

Rennie v. *Klein,* 462 Supp. 1131 (DNJ 1983) 476 F Supp 1294 (DNJ 1979) 9 FF'd in past, 653 F 2d 863 (3rd Cir 1981); 720 F 2d 266 13rd Cir 1983)

Rosenberg N: Law and the mental health system: the challenge of change, in Law and Ethics in the Practice of Psychiatry. Edited by Hofling C. New York, Brunner/Mazel, 1981

Rogers v. Commission, 458 NE 2d, 308 MASS, 1983

Rogers v. Okin, 478 F. Supp. 1342 (D. Mass. 1979)

Romeo v. Youngblood, 644 F. 2d 147 (1980)

Rouse v. Cameron, 373 F2d, 451 (D.C. Cir. 1966)

Runck B: Survey shows therapists misunderstand Tarasoff rule. Hosp Community Psychiatry 35(5):429-430, 1984

Slovenko R: Forensic psychiatry, in Comprehensive Textbook of Psychiatry. Kaplan HI, Freedman AM, Sadock BJ, Eds. Baltimore, Williams & Wilkins, 1980

Smith SM: Competency. Psychiatr Clin North America 6 (4):635-650, December 1983

Stone A: Recent mental health litigation: a critical perspective. Am J Psychiatry 134:273-279, 1977

Stone A: Law and psychiatry, in Psychiatry Update: The American Psychiatric Association Annual Review, Volume One. Edited by Grinspoon L. Washington, D.C., American Psychiatric Press, 1982

Stromberg C: Developments concerning the legal criteria for civil commitment: who are we looking for? in Psychiatry Update: The American Psychiatric Association Annual Review, Volume One. Edited by Grinspoon L. Washington, D. C., American Psychiatric Press, 1982

Tarasoff v. Regents of the University of California, 17, Cal 3d 425, 529, p2d 553 (1976)

Vitek v. Jones, 445 U.S. 480 (1980)

Walker N: Crime and Insanity in England, vol. 1. The Historical Perspective. Edinburgh, Edinburgh University Press, 1968

Weiner MF, Shuman DW: The privilege study. Arch Gen Psychiatry 40: 1027-1030, September 1983

Wyatt v. Stickney, 325 F. Supp. 781 (M.D. Ala. 1971a)

Yetter, 62 D C 619 (CP Northampton County, PA, 1973)

The Principle of Medical Ethics, with Annotations. Especially Applicable to Psychiatry, 1981 edition. Washington, D.C., American Psychiatric Association, 1981